Essential Equipment for the

Kitchen

A Sourcebook of the World's Best Designs

Published by Goodman Fiell, an imprint of
The Carlton Publishing Group
20 Mortimer Street
London, W1T 3JW

www.carltonbooks.co.uk

A CIP catalogue record for this book is available
from the British Library.

ISBN 978-1-84796-054-2

Text © 2013 Charlotte & Peter Fiell
Design © 2013 Goodman Fiell

Printed in China

<<< Lovisa Wattman, Model No. 4505 Collection
serving bowl for Höganäs Keramik, 1996

Mauviel Design Team, M'cook roasting pan
for Mauviel, 2003 >>>

Essential Equipment for the

Kitchen

A Sourcebook of the World's Best Designs

Charlotte & Peter Fiell

GOODMAN
FIELL

Contents

Introduction

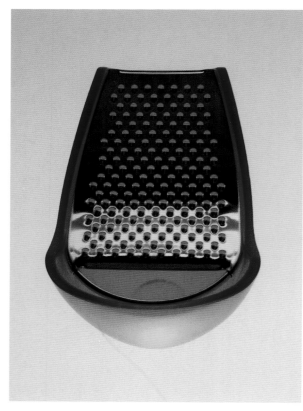

Alejandro Ruiz, *Parmenide* cheese grater for Alessi, 1994

Since prehistoric times, tools have shaped human existence. In fact the design, making and use of tools are distinguishing features of what it is to be human. Although other members of the animal kingdom fashion implements to assist them with certain limited tasks, no other species uses them to the same extraordinary extent. Indeed, it is no exaggeration to suggest that tools maketh man, because they allow us to shape the environments and cultures that make us who we are. Today our homes are literally crammed with tools, from kitchen knives to task lights, yet much of the stuff with which we surround ourselves is neither particularly well-designed nor especially well-made, because the market is frequently and predictably tethered to the commercial bottom line.

This book is based on the simple premise that well-designed objects can enhance our daily lives. We all need 'tools for living' – from cutlery and cooking utensils, to hobs and workstations– so this book focuses on the ultimate designs for the kitchen. After all, when you get right down to it, objects that fulfill the criteria for 'good design' are not only functionally and aesthetically superior, but they usually last longer too. Moreover, this enhanced durability is ultimately better for the environment. If a product lasts twice as long as its competitors then its net environmental impact is halved, so buying 'better' makes sound eco-sense as well as economic sense.

Well-designed objects are also more pleasurable to use; they give us joy by helping us to accomplish a specific task more rapidly and efficiently. They are also more likely to possess functional and structural integrity, which makes them less susceptible to the vagaries of fashion. The old saying 'buy cheap, buy twice' remains true, and we believe that it is preferable in the long run to buy an object that functions well because it has been carefully and painstakingly designed, even if it is a little more expensive. Cheaper, poor-quality versions are more likely to fail or to become stylistically obsolete – either way they will have to be replaced. By contrast, many of the designs selected for this survey could, with careful use, be passed down through generations of users because they have been designed to last.

Some of the items in this book are truly democratic and cost just a few pounds or dollars, others are more exclusive and cost several hundred or in a few cases several thousand. Regardless of price, though, they are all the best of their kind. Many are innovative products recently designed by today's leading talents, while others are acknowledged 'design classics' that have stood the test of time, such as David Mellor's *Pride* cutlery or Zeroll's ice cream scoop. We have also included historic designs that have been honed to functional perfection over decades, and in some cases over centuries, such as the traditional *Brown Betty* teapot.

Over the years, friends and family have repeatedly asked us, 'Where can I get really well-designed cutlery?', 'What is the best toaster?', 'Which serving bowls can you recommend?'. So we decided to make our selection of the best-designed kitchen products available, with the one proviso that any selected design has to be in current production so that it can be purchased. Each selection is accompanied with a short description of its attributes from a design perspective. We have also provided the manufacturers' web addresses, so that items can be sourced with relative ease. It has been an all-consuming search that has spanned the world of domestic tools, from Japanese knives and Finnish cooking pots to French storage jars and English teapots.

As Michael Landy's *Break Down* art installation in London (2001) emphatically revealed, the average home contains literally thousands of objects, many that are not particularly needed or even really wanted. Instead of endlessly accumulating domestic dross – from useless gadgets and kitsch gimmicks to knock-off 'designer' pastiches and furnishings so poorly made that they are only intended to last a few years – we should perhaps subscribe to the entreaty formulated by William Morris: 'Have nothing in your house that you do not know to be useful or believe to be beautiful'. Wouldn't it be better not to clutter our lives with a sea of questionable bric-a-brac, but rather to share our homes with a smaller number of functionally and aesthetically refined possessions?

Ernesto Rogers, the famous Milanese architect, believed that by studying a spoon it should be possible to understand the culture that had created it and to extrapolate the type of city that such a society would build. Surveying the plethora of shoddy household goods found in our stores today can hardly fill us with confidence about our present trajectory. Given the finite nature of the world's resources the time has surely come for responsible quality over mindless quantity. With dizzying speed the bling-tastic must-haves of the last decade have already become the tarnished junk of a past era marked by its celebrity obsessions and cultural emptiness. Instead there is a growing awareness and an increasing appreciation of 'ideal' objects that are functional, durable and timelessly beautiful. These are purposeful objects that inspire the mind, gladden the eye, warm the heart, and comfort the hand... objects that are cherished tools in the workshops of our daily lives.

One of the main ways we accumulate objects is through gifting, so another aim of this publication is to function as an essential guide and source of inspiration for people looking for that special present. An object for the kictehn or dining room that works well and looks beautiful can give years of pleasure to the recipient, which is a lot more than can be said for all those unwanted gifts of last resort. We equally hope that those setting out to equip their own homes will use this book to make informed choices. An inferior design often costs as much as a good one, and careful purchasing decisions will pay dividends in the present and in the future. Naturally, this book will also appeal to people who just want to buy the best, which, of course, doesn't necessarily mean the most expensive.

In Scandinavian countries it has long been believed that good design is the life-enhancing birthright of all. We hope that this guide to the world's best kitchen products and utensils will bring pleasure and enjoyment into our daily lives through better, more considered design.

CP-1ON peeler, 2002

Kyocera Design Team

www.kyocera.com
High-tech ceramic
Kyocera, Kyoto, Japan

The Japanese company Kyocera develops high-tech ceramics with a wide range of applications: from solar panels and semi-conductors to hip replacements and cutting tools, including various kitchen knives. They also manufacture the rustproof *CP-1ON* peeler, which comes in a variety of colours. Its advanced ceramic blade cuts smoothly and evenly, while holding its edge ten times longer than traditional metal peelers.

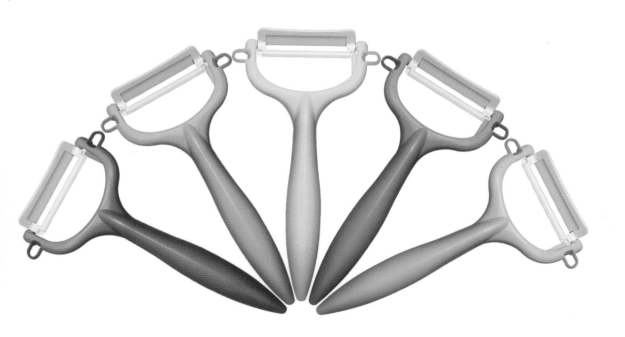

Rex Model 11002 peeler, 1947

Alfred Neweczeral (Switzerland, 1899–1958)

www.zena.ch
Aluminium, stainless-steel
↔ 10.9 cm
Zena, Affoltern, Switzerland

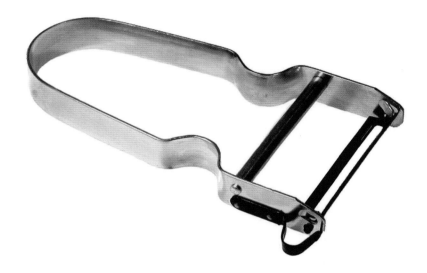

Acknowledged as a design classic in Switzerland, the *Rex* potato peeler has even been featured in a series of postage stamps celebrating iconic Swiss designs. Very affordable yet highly effective, this award-winning, easy-to-clean design is robust and stable, with two indentations that ensure a firm grip. It has the added benefit of being suitable for both right-handed and left-handed users.

Countertop garlic press, 2007

Cuisipro Design Team

www.cuisipro.com
Zinc alloy, thermoplastic
Cuisipro, Markham, Ontario, Canada

This ingenious, dishwasher-safe design has a non-slip base, which means that it can be pushed downwards onto a countertop if greater leverage is required. It can also, of course, be held in the hand when pressing garlic cloves. The garlic is squeezed through the hopper into a spoon-like collector built into the base, which can then be easily removed to transfer the freshly pressed garlic into a bowl or pan.

R 12782 garlic press, 2000

Rösle Design Team

www.roesle.de
Stainless steel
Rösle, Marktoberdorf, Germany

Although a touch more expensive than your average run-
of-the-mill garlic press, Rösle's r 12782 garlic press is easily
worth the extra cost, not least because its special levering
mechanism can even process unpeeled cloves. Easy to use
and easy to clean, this press is one of the company's most
popular designs, and reflects the German desire for superla-
tively engineered and rigorously functional products.

Good Grips Pro Y peeler & Good Grips Snap-Lock can opener, 1990 & 2003

Smart Design (USA, est. 1978)

www.oxo.com
Stainless steel, zinc, Santoprene/Santoprene, nylon, ABS, polypropylene, stainless steel
OXO International, New York (NY), USA

Every kitchen needs a well-designed can opener and vegetable peeler. They are essential tools for cooking, yet all too often one finds examples that are difficult, if not downright uncomfortable to use. The concept of 'good design' rests on the idea of fitness for purpose, and Smart Design's ergonomic approach to problem solving is certainly in harmony with this outlook. This results in the creation of better tools, such as these soft-gripped yet sturdy designs.

Good Grips Pro Swivel peeler & Good Grips Pro jar opener, 2003

Smart Design (USA, est. 1978)

www.oxo.com
Stainless steel, Santoprene, polypropylene, die-cast zinc/stainless steel, Santoprene, polypropylene, ABS, TPE
OXO International, New York (NY), USA

Smart Design works from a holistic standpoint in order to create responsible designs that humanize technology and foster an emotional connection with their users. Through the success of their numerous kitchenware designs for OXO, this New York-based office has tirelessly promoted the idea of 'inclusive design', such as this user-friendly jar opener and soft-grip peeler.

Bistro herb chopper, 2007

Bodum Design Group

www.bodum.com
Acrylic, non-slip rubber, stainless steel
Bodum, Triengen, Switzerland

Winning a prestigious Red Dot award in 2007, the *Bistro*
herb chopper is a compact design that performs excellently.
It allows you to chop herbs like a professional but – thanks
to its seven stainless-steel, double-edged, rotary blades –
with minimal effort. In addition, the flower-shaped cap
enhances the grip, while the transparent base means that
the progress of your herbs can be monitored mid-chop.

Parmenide cheese grater, 1994

Alejandro Ruiz (Argentina, 1954–)

www.alessi.com
PMMA, stainless steel
Alessi, Crusinallo, Italy

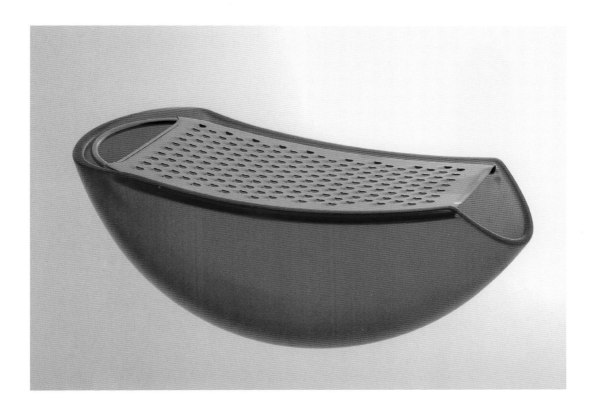

This cheese grater, like so many designs produced by Alessi, is not only aesthetically pleasing but also works exceptionally well. A translucent plastic compartment, that looks like a turtle's back, catches the grated Parmesan cheese as it falls, so that it can be sprinkled directly onto your food or stored for later use. In addition, the stainless-steel grating section can be effortlessly removed for easy cleaning. A stylish design, the *Parmenide* offers a no-mess solution at an affordable price.

Gourmet 45000 Series graters, 2008

Microplane International Design Team

www.microplaneintl.com
Chemically photo-etched stainless steel, thermoplastic
Microplane International, Russellville (AR), USA

In 1990, Richard and Jeff Grace invented a new tool, the Microplane rasp, with chemically photo-etched, razor-like edges. Three years later, a Canadian homemaker, Lorraine Lee, was baking and used her husband's new rasp to grate an orange. To her amazement, 'lacy shards of zest fell from its surface like snowflakes'. Using the same technology, and achieving the same excellent results, the *Microplane Gourmet* series has six options, from fine through to extra-coarse grating and shaving.

Accutec flat grater, 2002

Cuisipro Design Team

www.cuisipro.com
Stainless steel, elastomer
Cuisipro, Markham, Ontario, Canada

Cuisipro manufactures a range of four flat graters with different gauges depending on the kind of food you need to process. The fine version is perfect for citrus zest or for grating Parmesan cheese, while the ultra-coarse grater can handle softer cheeses such as cheddar or even mozzarella. These razor-sharp graters have larger-than-average grating surfaces, and also boast non-slip feet to provide stability when they are used angled against a countertop.

95020 grater, 2000
Rösle Design Team

www.roesle.de
Stainless steel
Rösle, Marktoberdorf, Germany

In 1888, a master tinsmith named Karl Theodor Rösle established a company in southern Germany producing roofing components. However, in 1903 the firm diversified into the production of kitchen utensils, and today, Rösle manufactures some of the finest kitchen utensils available. The grater shown here incorporates advanced laser-welding technologies first developed for the automotive industry, which allow the company to deliver higher quality in manufacturing, while also improving hygiene.

Profi Tools grater, 2007

Peter Ramminger (Germany, 1962–)

www.wmf.de
Cromargan stainless steel, thermoplastic
WMF Württembergische Metallwarenfabrik, Geislingen, Germany

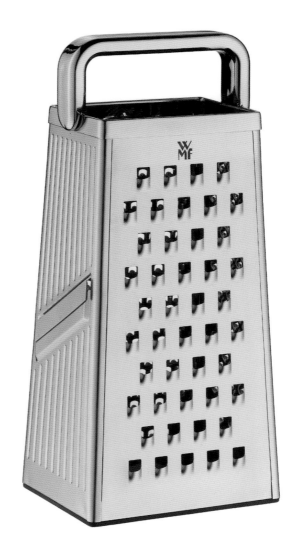

A member of WMF's in-house design team since 1999, Peter Ramminger believes design to be, 'the challenge of creating products which enhance each day by making things easier'. His four-sided grater is testament to this idea. Almost razor sharp, the design incorporates a cucumber slicer, fine and coarse vegetable graters, and also a potato grater. It comes with a handy removable plastic base, and a stable handle that ensures a safe grip.

Accutec three-sided box grater, 2002

Cuisipro Design Team

www.cuisipro.com
Stainless steel, elastomer
Cuisipro, Markham, Ontario, Canada

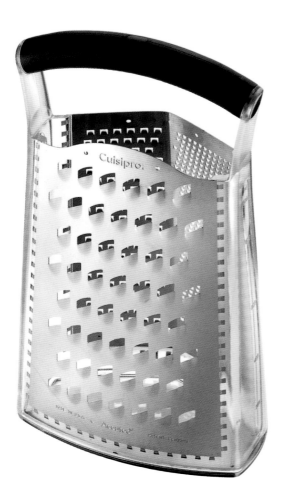

The razor-sharp *Accutec* grater has three grating surfaces – ultra-coarse, coarse and fine – which comprise double-sided, acid-etched blades that can cope with virtually any food products, from soft cheeses and vegetables to chocolate and citrus fruit. With its easy-to-grip handle, its non-slip removable base that catches the grated food, and the handy calibrated measurements displayed on one of its sides, this dishwasher-safe design provides superior performance at little extra cost.

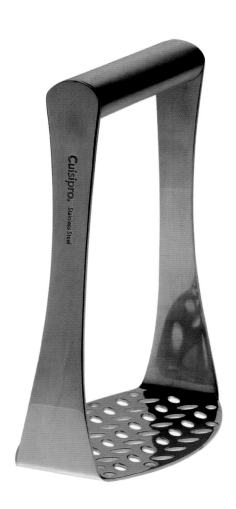

Potato masher, 2000

Cuisipro Design Team

www.cuisipro.com
Stainless steel
Cuisipro, Markham, Ontario, Canada

The large handle of this heavy-duty, dish-washer-safe, stainless-steel potato masher provides an excellent grip, and ensures efficient mashing. The handle's high position also keeps the hand safely away from the steaming boiled potatoes, while the holes are designed and positioned to give a lump-free result. Cuisipro also produces a similar design in a lightweight but strong reinforced thermoplastic.

Z-Gadget apple corer, 2007
RSVP International Design Team

www.rsvp-intl.com
Chrome-plated zinc alloy
RSVP International, Seattle (WA), USA

RSVP International is a Seattle-based manufacturer of durable, high-quality kitchen items, which are stamped with a reassuring American robustness, both in their design and construction. RSVP's *Z-Gadget* apple corer is, as its name suggests, a sturdy, heavyweight design that slices apples with ease and that should survive a lifetime of use.

All Professional large pizza cutter, c. 2000

All-Clad Metalcrafters Design Team

www.all-clad.com
Stainless steel
All-Clad Metalcrafters, Canonsburg (PA), USA

The downward pressure exerted on a pizza cutter can be quite significant, so it is a good idea to find a design that is really sturdy. All-Clad prides itself on the fact that its *All Professional* range of products are built to last, and certainly this stainless-steel pizza cutter offers excellent performance thanks to its superior strength, while also being comfortable to handle.

O-Series scissors, 1963–1967 (original design)

Olof Bäckström (Norway, 1922–)

www.fiskars.com
Stainless steel, ABS
Fiskars, Fiskars, Finland

In 1967, Fiskars launched its famous orange-handled scissors. They had been developed by a Norwegian engineer, Olof Bäckström, who had painstakingly carved prototypes of the handles from solid wood to ensure they were as ergonomically resolved as possible. With their ABS handles, the subsequent production models fit beautifully in the hand, and are also available in left-handed versions. Dishwasher-proof and highly durable, these iconic scissors will last a lifetime and are a joy to use on each and every occasion.

Twin Select kitchen shears, 2003–2004

Zwilling JA Henckels Design Team

www.zwilling.com
Stainless steel
Zwilling JA Henckels, Solingen, Germany

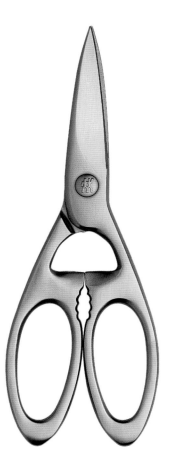

Founded in Solingen in 1731, Henckels is now renowned worldwide for its superlative knives and scissors, which epitomize the high-quality craftsmanship and design that have come to characterize the label 'Made in Germany'. The company's *Twin Select* series was first introduced in 2001, and includes these useful multipurpose kitchen shears. Their micro-serrated blades can be used to cut virtually anything, from cardboard and string to flowers and silk.

95622 French whisk, 1978

Rösle Design Team

www.roesle.de
Stainless steel
Rösle, Marktoberdorf, Germany

Rösle makes every imaginable kind of kitchen implement, including nineteen different types of whisk – some are designed to beat eggs, some are balloon whisks for aerating and mixing batters, and others are specifically designed to be used in conjunction with a jug rather than a bowl. Their 'French' whisk, shown here, is not only perfectly balanced and easy to use, but is a beautiful object in its own right, thanks to Rösle's form-follows-function approach to design.

1000 Rondy egg slicer, 1960s

Famos-Westmark Design Team

www.westmark.de
Aluminium, stainless-steel wires
Famos-Westmark, Lennestadt, Germany

This restaurant-quality egg slicer has separately mounted, tensioned, stainless-steel wires, and can be used to produce round or oval egg slices. Like so many household products manufactured in Germany, the *1000 Rondy* is a no-nonsense practical design, and is extremely well made. Highly durable and functionally successful, it should also considerably outlast similar products thanks to its superior build quality.

Endurance egg topper, 2000

RSVP International Design Team

www.rsvp-intl.com
Stainless steel
RSVP International, Seattle, USA

Constructed of high-quality stainless steel, the *Endurance* egg topper is a handy device for people who love boiled eggs but hate peeling eggshell. Basically, you pop the 'topper' on a boiled egg, squeeze its handles together and a ring of teeth pierces the top of the egg: hey presto, your egg is ready to eat, and free of annoying pieces of shell.

A, B, C... cutlery tray, 1996

Jasper Morrison (UK, 1959–)

www.magisdesign.com
Polypropylene
↔ 34.5 cm ↕ 28.5 cm
Magis, Motta di Livenza, Italy

From the *Magis Accessories Collection*, Jasper
Morrison's *A, B, C...* cutlery tray epitomizes
both his essentialist approach to design and
the aesthetic and functional purity of his work.
This design is an outgrowth of his 'super normal'
philosophy, which holds that, 'the super normal
object is the result of a long tradition of evolutionary advancement in the shape of everyday
things, not attempting to break with the history
of form but rather trying to summarize it,
knowing its place in the society of things.'

Funnel, 2004

Boje Estermann (Denmark, 1961–)

www.normann-copenhagen.com
Santoprene
⌀ 12 cm
Normann Copenhagen, Copenhagen, Denmark

This dishwasher-safe, space-saving and award-winning funnel is made from a specially developed flexible rubber. As Boje Estermann explains, 'I got inspired to design the funnel during my final assignment at the School of Design in Paris. The main idea was to develop items that didn't take up space in the kitchen. A funnel is a product that can be annoying when not in use, mainly because it takes up space and you can't stack it…The idea for the folding funnel was originally inspired by my old camera.'

Measuring cup set, 2004

All-Clad Metalcrafters Design Team

www.all-clad.com
Stainless steel
All-Clad Metalcrafters, Canonsburg (PA), USA

Every cook needs a set of measuring cups, especially if they are using a North American recipe book, and the ones manufactured by All-Clad Metalcrafters are of premium quality. This five-piece set is made from high-grade $^{18}/_{10}$ stainless steel, and unlike most on the market this set has angled handles that make the cups easier to hold when measuring out dry or liquid ingredients. Like other cooking equipment produced by All-Clad Metalcrafters, these measuring cups are robust enough to last a lifetime.

Tape Timer kitchen timer, 2004

Jozeph Forakis (USA, 1962–)

www.kikkerland.com
Aluminium, polycarbonate, ABS
↕ 10.2 cm
Kikkerland Design, New York (NY), USA

Inspired by a carpenter's measuring tape, this ticking
kitchen timer is operated using a pull-ring to extend
the tape to the required length of time. *Tape Timer* was
based on the years of research Jozeph Forakis has devoted
on 'interaction design', and the idea of user experience.
According to Forakis, this approach aims to develop a new
'aesthetics of behaviour', which offers a fresh take on products we often take for granted.

Mini Timer, 1971

Richard Sapper (Germany, 1932–)

www.terraillon.com
ABS
↔ 2.9 cm   ⌀ 6.7 cm
Terraillon, Chatou Cedex, France

Following the astonishing sales success of Terraillon's BA 2000 kitchen scales, Richard Sapper went on to design a complementary kitchen-timer for the French company. With its colourful plastic surfaces and bold geometric form, the diminutive yet useful *Mini Timer* possesses a pared-down aesthetic that epitomises 1970s Pop-Minimalism.

BA 2000 kitchen scale, 1969-1970

Marco Zanuso (Italy, 1916–2001) & Richard Sapper (Germany, 1932–)

www.terraillon.fr
PMMA, ABS
↕ 17 cm ↔ 13 cm ⤢ 11 cm
Terraillon, Chatou, France

Sleek and compact, the BA 2000 kitchen scales have a bowl (suitable for measuring dry ingredients or liquids) that can be inverted to form a flat-topped lid for easy storage. When first launched in the early 1970s, this classic design became an instant bestseller in France, thanks to its unusual Pop-meets-Bauhaus aesthetic and excellent functionality – which includes an angled magnifying lens that makes the dial easy to read from a counter-top position.

Bistro kitchen scale, 2006

Bodum Design Group

www.bodum.com
Various materials
↔ 19.7 cm ↕ 17 cm
Bodum, Triengen, Switzerland

Thanks to its integrated functionality and minimalist aesthetic, this compact digital kitchen scale won a Good Design award, an iF design award and a Red Dot award in 2007. It operates using metric or imperial units of measurement, and also incorporates a tare function that means additional items can be weighed separately. Although relatively small, this wipe-clean scale will weigh amounts up to five kilogrammes, and its cover doubles up as a bowl.

Full Scale kitchen scale, 2002

Hendrik Holbæk (Denmark, 1960–) & Claus Jensen (Denmark, 1966–)

www.evasolo.com
Stainless steel, glass
1 kg
Eva Solo, Maaloev, Denmark

This ingenious kitchen scale will weigh amounts up to one kilogramme. It is dishwasher-safe and can also be used as a measuring jug. In addition, it has a tare function, which means that it can be zeroed back to weigh additional items, and it is inscribed with metric, imperial and US measuring units. Redefining the humble kitchen scale, this design received various accolades in 2002, including a Form award, an Excellence in Housewares award and a Red Dot award.

Hot Pot Gourmet measuring jug, 2002

Bodum Design Group

www.bodum.com
Borosilicate glass
0.5 l, 1 l
Bodum, Triengen, Switzerland

Dishwasher-proof and microwave-safe, the *Hot Pot Gourmet* measuring jug is a practical kitchen tool that epitomizes the democratic approach to design promoted by Bodum. Although originally founded in Denmark, the company relocated to Switzerland in 1980, and its in-house design unit, known as PI-Design, was formed that same year. Since then, the company has produced literally hundreds of household designs that conform to its motto: 'excellent design has to be affordable to anyone'.

Pyrex measuring jugs, 1920s (original design)

Corning Design Team

www.pyrex.com
Pyrex®
0.5 l, 1.0 l
Corning, Corning (NY), USA

No kitchen should be without a *Pyrex* measuring jug – they are just so useful and versatile. Available in a range of sizes and styles, they are highly durable thanks to the thermal shock resistance and sturdy strength of their borosilicate glass. These products have the added benefit of not absorbing flavours, odours or stains, and they also come with easy-to-read metric, imperial and cup measurements. Moreover, they are oven, microware and freezer safe.

Good Grips salad spinner, 1998

OXO Design Team

www.oxo.com
Thermoplastic, Santoprene
⌀ 25.4 cm
OXO International, New York (NY), USA

Salad spinners are often quite hard to control, even for the physically able. But imagine trying to keep one stable if you had arthritic hands – it would be a nightmare, and probably a mess too. The *Good Grips* salad spinner addresses this problem by incorporating a non-slip ring, and also a soft elastomer knob that permits a simple, one-handed operation of the spinner.

Good Grips convertible colander, 2005

Bally Design (USA, est. 1972)

www.oxo.com
Stainless steel, thermoplastic
4.73 l
OXO International, New York (NY), USA

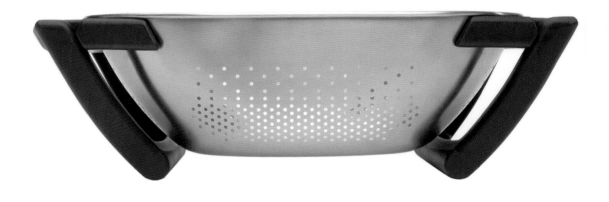

OXO produces affordable, high quality and 'inclusive'
kitchenware designs. Their products are also frequently
functionally innovative. This colander, for instance, has
handles that allow it to be carried safely, yet those same
handles can be folded down to create leg-like rests to
support the colander, thereby protecting whatever surface
it is placed upon – a simple and ingenious solution.

23120 colander, 1989

Rösle Design Team

www.roesle.de
Stainless steel
11.8 l
Rösle, Marktoberdorf, Germany

Available in three sizes, this generous colander with its distinctive, beaded edge has perforations on its base and sides to ensure quick and efficient drainage. Its two sturdy handles make it easy to carry, while its large capacity is perfect for washing, draining or straining larger quantities of food. It is such a beautiful design that it seems to transcend its simple everyday function.

23218 conical strainer & 95190 strainer, 1980

Rösle Design Team

www.roesle.de
Stainless steel
1.5 l, 1.25 l
Rösle, Marktoberdorf, Germany

Never underestimate the simple pleasure of using a well-designed strainer that drains quickly and rinses easily. These strainers made by Rösle are exquisitely crafted, and their perfect balance makes them easy to handle. They come in a number of sizes, and have the added advantage of being completely dishwasher-proof. The mesh version is intended for straining sauces or soups, while the other is perfect for straining vegetables, rice or pasta.

Endurance Precision Pierced colander, 2003

RSVP International Design Team

www.rsvp-intl.com
Stainless steel
2.8 l, 4.7 l
RSVP International, Seattle (WA), USA

With its precision piercing, this colander drains away surplus water quickly and easily. At the same time, though, its holes are small enough to hold back particles of rice, orzo, couscous or quinoa. Sturdy but light, this easy-to-clean design was voted a favourite by *Cook's Illustrated* magazine, and has received numerous complimentary reviews from users.

Stainless-steel bowls & strainers, 1960

Sori Yanagi (Japan, 1915–)

www.gatewayjapan.dk
Stainless steel
∅ 13, 16, 19, 23, 27 cm (bowls)
∅ 16, 19, 23, 27 cm (strainers)
Sori Yanagi, Valby, Denmark

For centuries, the idea of functional simplicity has guided the arts and crafts of Japan, a preoccupation closely linked to the striking aesthetic purity of so much Japanese design. Sori Yanagi's kitchen accessories, such as these stainless-steel bowls and strainers, stand as testament to the vitality of this absorbing design heritage. Like traditional Japanese household wares, these beautiful 'tools' are a joy to use because of the thought and craftsmanship that has informed their design and manufacture.

Margrethe mixing bowls, 1950

Sigvard Bernadotte (Sweden, 1907–2002) & Acton Bjørn (Denmark, 1910–1992)

www.rosti-housewares.dk
Melamine, rubber
1.5 l, 2 l, 3 l, 4 l
Rosti Housewares, Ebeltoft, Denmark

Born into the Swedish royal family, Count Sigvard Bernadotte designed numerous innovative products, many of
them in collaboration with his Danish colleague, Acton
Bjørn. The *Margrethe* melamine mixing bowls – their
response to a brief to design the 'ideal mixing bowl' – are
produced in a number of bright colours. These sturdily
sculptural nesting bowls have non-slip rubber bases, as
well as highly practical pouring spouts and useful hand-
grips. The bowls were named after Count Bernadotte's
niece, Princess Margrethe, now the sovereign of Denmark.

Pyrex mixing bowl set, c.1915 (original design)

Corning Design Team

www.pyrex.com
Pyrex®
⌀ 14, 16, 21, 24 cm
Corning, Corning (NY), USA

The famous Corning glassworks developed a heat-resistant
borosilicate glass in the late 1880s, and in 1911 the company
adjusted its formula so that it would be suitable for the
manufacture of kitchenware. This new glass was named
Pyrex® and in 1915 a range of Pyrex-branded cookware
was launched with the motto 'glass dishes for baking'. For
over ninety years, the design of these classic, stacking
Pyrex mixing bowls has altered little – a testament to the
relevance and usefulness of the concept.

15320 mixing bowl, 1987

Rösle Design Team

www.roesle.de
Stainless steel
1.48 l, 2.75 l, 4.76 l
Rösle, Marktoberdorf, Germany

The design of this mixing bowl has been informed by
a careful analysis of function. The integrated grip and
thumb-ring give the user a firm hold, which is essential
when beating egg whites, stirring sauces or making salad
dressings. The lipped rim ensures drip-free pouring, while
the overall tilt of the bowl makes the act of mixing easier – a
beautiful example of form following function.

Versalid bowl set, 1995

Rösle Design Team

www.roesle.de
Stainless steel
1.16 l, 2.43 l, 4.23 l
Rösle, Marktoberdorf, Germany

This multi-functional covered bowl can be used for food preparation, marinating, defrosting, storing or even serving at a table. The lid also has an integrated stainless-steel vent that can either be tightly sealed for the transportation of food or opened for ventilation in order to let food breathe. The bowl's unusual asymmetrical rim was designed for efficient pouring of liquids.

Good Grips rolling pin, 2001

Smart Design (USA, est. 1978)

www.oxo.com
Thermoplastic
OXO International, New York (NY), USA

Thinking of making cookies or pies? If so, every homemaker needs a good rolling pin that will roll out the dough or pastry uniformly and evenly. Unfortunately, however, most rolling pins are not ergonomically refined, which means that the elderly, and those suffering from arthritis, often find them difficult to use. The exception is the *Good Grips* rolling pin. Its contoured and weighted handles are designed so that hands and knuckles are kept in an optimum raised position, and as such do not painfully hit counter tops when rolling out.

Good Grips pastry brush, 2006

Smart Design (USA, est. 1978)

www.oxo.com
Thermoplastic, silicone
OXO International, New York (NY), USA

Unlike old-fashioned wooden and bristle pastry brushes, the *Good Grips* version does not clump together, nor does it retain clinging food odours. It can also be placed in the dishwasher and, thanks to its use of silicone for its bristles, it is heat-resistant up to 315 °C (600 °F). Made from an elastomeric polymer, the handle also provides a comfortably soft grip making it easier to use.

Good Grips trivet & oven mitt, 2008

Smart Design (USA, est. 1978)

www.oxo.com
Silicone/Silicone, fabric, magnet
oxo International, New York (NY), USA

This trivet and matching oven mitt incorporate high-grade silicone, which is heat-resistant up to an impressive 315°c (600°f). The trivet also doubles up as a useful potholder, while the oven mitt has a thick, multi-layer liner that gives additional thermal insulation. The mitt really fits like a proper glove and its ribbed design provides a secure grip. It also has a long sleeve option to protect the wrist and forearm from accidental burns.

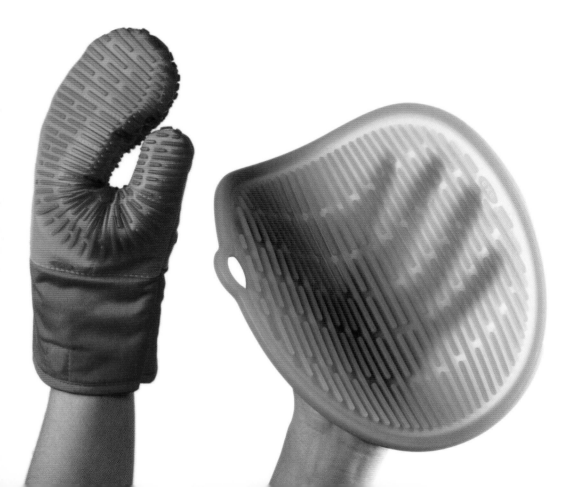

Good Grips spatula, 2007

Smart Design (USA, est. 1978)

www.oxo.com
Wood, silicone
oxo International, New York City (NY), USA

Like other kitchen tools concieved by Smart Design for oxo's ubiquitous Good Grips range, this spatula is an 'inclusive design', which can be used by most members of society regardless of age or physical ability. Although at first glance it looks like almost any other spatula, the design's large solid wooden handle has been ergonomically shaped to fit the hand. It therefore has a comfortable and stable grip for stirring or scraping. The heat-resistant silicone head can also be removed for cleaning.

Edge chopping block & breadboard, 2005

Pascal Charmolu (France, 1958–)

www.sagaform.com
Oiled oak
↕ 10 cm   ↔ 30.5 cm   ↗ 30.5 cm
↔ 45 cm   ↗ 22.5 cm
Sagaform, Borås, Sweden

Although a French citizen, Pascal Charmolu studied at the Swedish Academy of Arts and Crafts in Stockholm – a city that has since been his home for more than twenty-five years. During this time he has worked as a freelance designer, receiving numerous awards for his innovative product design solutions. Charmolu has also worked extensively for Sagaform designing, for instance, this sturdy and distinctive chopping block and breadboard.

Edge cheeseboard, 2005

Pascal Charmolu (France, 1958–)

www.sagaform.com
Oiled oak, glass
↕ 45 cm ↔ 22.5 cm
Sagaform, Borås, Sweden

Pascal Charmolu's *Edge* cheeseboard innovatively and seamlessly combines wood with glass to create a design that can be used for cutting bread and serving cheese: perfect for buffets, suppers or dinner parties. Like other Sagaform products, the *Edge* cheeseboard has a Scandinavian simplicity that provides affordable 'good design' for the home.

Mingle Lazy Susan cheeseboard, 2005

Peter Moritz (Sweden, 1964–) & Eva Moritz (Sweden, 1966–)

www.sagaform.com
Walnut, painted trim
↕ 25.5 cm ↔ 25.5 cm
Sagaform, Borås, Sweden

The term 'Lazy Susan', used to describe a rotating tabletop tray, was first used in an advertisement from 1917 in *Vanity Fair* magazine, and presumably alluded to an idle servant. Certainly a useful device for serving, the Lazy Susan concept has now been reinterpreted by Peter and Eva Moritz in their *Mingle* cheeseboard. Made from subtly grained walnut, its richly coloured surface is ideal for presenting a selection of cheeses.

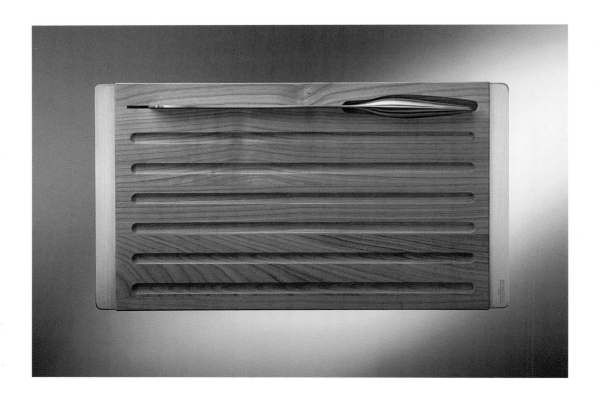

570 breadboard with knife, 2007

Peter Sägesser (Switzerland, 1952–)

www.saegiag.ch
Cherry or maple, stainless steel
↕ 3 cm ↔ 42 cm ⤢ 24 cm
Sägi, Zurich, Switzerland

Mirroring the national characteristics of order and calm,
Swiss-designed products for the home have a reassuring yet
understated presence; they do the job well, but don't feel
the need to shout about it. The Zurich-based company, Sägi,
manufactures products that epitomise Swiss designers'
logical yet thoughtful approach to design, such as this beautifully made breadboard.

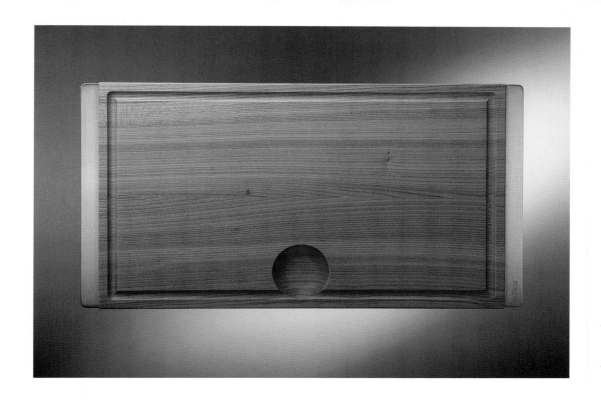

560 chopping board, 2007

Peter Sägesser (Switzerland, 1952–)

www.saegiag.ch
Cherrywood or maple, stainless steel
↕ 3 cm ↔ 49.5 cm ⤢ 26 cm
Sägi, Zurich, Switzerland

Swiss Design is generally characterised by a functional
clarity and an extraordinary level of detail, as can be seen in
Peter Sägesser's 560 chopping board with its stainless steel
handles. This simple yet logical design reflects the desire for
superior kitchenwares in Switzerland, a country long famed
for its culinary arts and teaching. It also reveals the nation's
appreciation of high-quality and perfectly engineered
designs that will last a lifetime.

Shun Pro 2 kitchen knives, 2005

Ken Onion (USA, 1963–) & Alton Brown (USA, 1962–)

www.kershawknives.com
Steel, stainless steel, pakkawood, brass
Kershaw Knives/Kai USA, Tualatin (OR), USA

Although designed and manufactured in America, these super-sharp knives employ an age-old Japanese knife-making technique known as *honyaki*, in which the blade is made from a single piece of high-grade steel. The design also employs the Japanese *kasumi* method, which involves cladding the steel blades with a protective layer of stainless steel and then burnishing it so that – like a *Samurai* sword – they not only have a superior cutting edge but also bear a distinctive Damascene wavy pattern.

Global G-8311/K kitchen knife set, 1983

Komin Yamada (Japan, 1947–)

www.yoshikin.co.jp
Stainless steel
Yoshida Metal Industry Company, Yoshida, Japan

When Komin Yamada's *Global* knife range was launched in 1983, it established a new standard for all-stainless-steel, one-piece knife construction. With their cleverly integrated handles and blades, *Global* knives have excellent cutting and handling characteristics, and they look really good too, with their distinctive and very stylish black-pocked handles. The knife set shown here includes various slicing and chopping tools for preparing fish, meat and vegetables, and for cutting bread.

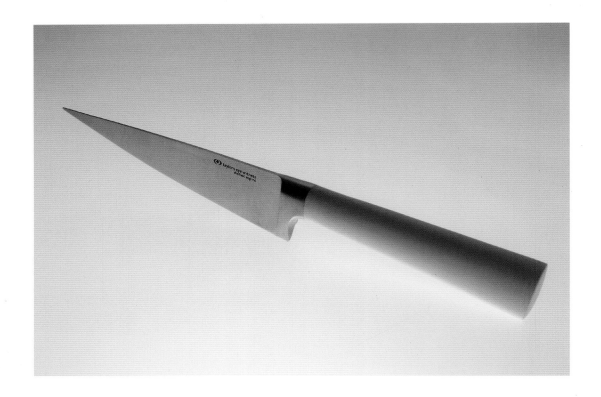

IF4000 knives, 2004

Industrial Facility/Sam Hecht (UK, 1969–) & Kim Colin (USA, 1961–)

www.taylors-eye-witness.co.uk
Stainless steel, ceramic, polyester
Taylor's Eye Witness, Sheffield, UK

Having manufactured knives in Sheffield – England's historic steelmaking centre – for over 150 years, Taylor's Eye Witness commissioned Industrial Facility to design a new range of kitchen knives. The resulting *IF4000* range employs cool-to-the-touch 'advanced ceramic' handles, and high-grade stainless-steel blades that have both strength and flexibility. Winning a Design Plus award and also a gold iF award, this useful and beautiful kitchen knife collection is a veritable classic of contemporary British design.

Professional S knives, 1988–1989

Zwilling JA Henckels Design Team

www.zwilling.com
Solid steel, plastic
Zwilling JA Henckels, Solingen, Germany

In 1731, the knife maker Peter Henckels registered his famous 'twin' symbol with the Cutlers' Guild in Solingen. Since then, this trademark has become a signifier of product excellence. With solid, all-steel blades and seamless, riveted handles, the *Professional S* range of forty-six knives, designed for every conceivable culinary need, are a favourite among professional chefs, who know they can rely on these superior cutting tools.

Model 130 Professional Sharpening Station knife sharpener, 2005

Dan Friel Sr (USA, 1920–)

www.edgecraft.com
Various materials
↔ 24.8 cm
Chef's Choice/EdgeCraft, Avondale (PA), USA

Available in four finishes, the user-friendly *Model 130* is a compact professional knife sharpening unit, which uses a three-stage system to sharpen any type of knife you can imagine – from straight-edged to serrated. The first stage uses diamond abrasives to sharpen the edge of the knife, the second stage incorporates a super-hardened steel to create a superior cutting edge, and the final stage employs a flexible stropping disk to polish the edge to 'hair-splitting sharpness'.

Chantry Modern Knife Sharpener, 2004

Industrial Facility/Sam Hecht (UK, 1969–) & Kim Colin (USA, 1961–)

www.taylors-eye-witness.co.uk
Enamelled metal, spring-loaded steels
↔ 20 cm
Taylor's Eye Witness, Sheffield, UK

Sam Hecht is renowned for his simple yet logical products that innovatively update existing typologies. A prime example is his *Chantry Modern Knife Sharpener* for Taylor's Eye Witness, a Sheffield-based manufacturer that has been making superior-quality knives since 1838. This award-winning design incorporates the company's existing chantry device (two small, spring-loaded butchers' steels positioned at the optimum angle) within a clean-lined and practical knife sharpener.

Good Grips kitchen tools, 1996

Smart Design (USA, est. 1978)

www.oxo.com
Polyamide
OXO International, New York (NY), USA

Smart Design has created literally hundreds of designs for OXO, all of which have an inclusive remit that means they are suitable for most users regardless of physical ability. Apart from this ethical dimension, *Good Grips* products, including this extensive range of kitchen tools, also offer high performance and durability at an affordable price, thereby exemplifying the long-held and democratic notion of 'good design' for all.

Good Grips spaghetti servers & wooden spoons, & Good Grips salad servers, 2003–2004 & 2006

Smart Design (USA, est. 1978)

www.oxo.com
Beech
OXO International, New York (NY), USA

Made of solid beech, these sturdy wooden tools are both durable and comfortable to hold. They also have the added benefit of being safe to use with non-stick cookware. The elegant yet no-nonsense salad servers have large contoured handles and flared tines that ensure they are perfect not only for tossing a salad, but for serving and scooping at almost any angle. They exemplify elegant and inclusive design intended to enhance the art of living.

Good Grips serving spatula, 1999

Smart Design (USA, est. 1978)

www.oxo.com
Stainless steel, Santoprene
OXO International, New York City (NY), USA

With its soft, tapering handle made of Santoprene – a thermoplastic elastomer (in other
words a synthetic rubber) – this implement is
easy to use and is perfect for serving an array
of different dishes, from fruit pies to lasagne.
Dishwasher-safe and highly robust, it is absolutely perfect for everyday family meals, while
sufficiently elegant to bring out when enter-
taining guests.

All-Professional kitchen tool set, 1999

All-Clad Metalcrafters Design Team

www.all-clad.com
Stainless steel
All-Clad Metalcrafters,
Canonsburg (PA), USA

All-Clad's *All-Professional* kitchen tool set comprises the five most essential kitchen implements: a large spoon, a large fork, a ladle, a draining spoon and a spatula. The company, however, also manufactures a host of other tools that similarly feature All-Clad's distinctive and ergonomic stainless-steel handles. These high-quality and durable kitchen tools absolutely epitomize the no-nonsense robustness of American design and manufacture.

Kitchen utensils with hooks, 1993

Rösle Design Team

www.roesle.de
Stainless steel
Rösle, Marktoberdorf, Germany

Probably the most comprehensive range of kitchen utensils you can buy, Rösle's series of 'hooked' tools and complimentary racks combines no-nonsense practicality with high-quality manufacture. The range comprises twenty-five utensils, from skimmers and ladles to sausage lifters and spaghetti spoons. Like other Rösle products, these designs have each undergone a rigorous one or two-year development phase to ensure that they meet the exacting demands of the professional sector.

Kitchen tools, 1997–2000

Sori Yanagi (Japan, 1915–)

www.gatewayjapan.dk
Stainless steel
Sori Yanagi, Valby, Denmark

Combining functionality with an innate artistry, Sori Yanagi's simple objects possess a rare poetic beauty that elevates the aesthetic standards of homewares. His *Kitchen Tools* range (which includes ladles, a skimmer, turners, and tongs) is produced in the Niigata region of Japan, long famed as a centre for superlative metalworking. Winning the Japanese Good Design Award in 1998, these elegant objects epitomize Yanagi's goal: 'Japanese Design. Universal Use.'

16860 splatter guard, 2002

Rösle Design Team

www.roesle.de
Stainless steel
⌀ 26, 30, 33.5 cm
Rösle, Marktoberdorf, Germany

This splatter guard is made of high-grade stainless steel, and comes in three different sizes. Like other Rösle kitchenwares, many of which have won awards for their design innovation, this simple tool is extremely well made and is driven by practical considerations – in this case, the long handle keeps hands at a safe distance from hot pans. Unlike inferior designs on the market, this splatter guard will not tarnish or warp, and can also be cleaned easily.

Titanium 2000 Plus non-stick frying pan, 1997–1998

SKK Design Team

www.skk-guss.de
Titanium, stainless steel, aluminium
Ø 20, 24, 28, 32, 36, 40 cm
SKK Küchen-und Gasgeräte, Viersen-Boisheim, Germany

This professional frying pan is made from hand-cast
aluminium and has a titanium-reinforced, non-stick
surface that contributes to its exemplary performance
in the kitchen. Its specially developed 'thermocore' base
means that it can be used on electric rings, gas hobs or
even Aga-style hot plates (the exception being induction
hobs). The stainless-steel handle of this design is also
heat-resistant, which means that this stylish frying pan can
also be placed in an oven to keep food warm. The *Titanium
2000 Plus* is offered in six different pan sizes, and with three
different options for handle length.

Diamant 3000 Plus square grill pan, 2005

SKK Design Team

www.skk-guss.de
Titanium, stainless steel, Bakelite
↔ 26 cm
SKK Küchen-und Gasgeräte, Viersen-Boisheim, Germany

Made from cast aluminium, this professional grill pan boasts
a thick, four-layer, non-stick coating both inside and out.
As a result, it will not only last a good deal longer than most
competing designs on the market, but it will also remain
easy to clean. In addition, this useful, high-sided design has
a removable handle and a thick base which, unlike cheaper
versions, does not deform at high temperatures. Furthermore, the superior manufacture of this pan ensures even
heat distribution and enhanced cooking performance.

Diamant 3000 Plus grill pan, 2005

SKK Design Team

www.skk-guss.de
Titanium, stainless steel, Bakelite
↔ 24 cm
SKK Küchen-und Gasgeräte, Viersen-Boisheim, Germany

This German-made grill pan possesses a reassuring, non-nonsense robustness. Unlike most non-stick pans, this model can even be used with metal utensils because of its tough, four-layer 'Titanium 4000' coating. Because the food does not stick readily to the pan's surface, it also means less oil or fat is needed for cooking. The design also has a removable handle, so the pan can be put in an oven to keep its contents warm.

American square grill pan, 2005

Francis Staub (France, active 1970s–2000s)

www.staub.fr
Enamelled cast iron
↔ 30 cm
Staub, Turckheim, France

Staub manufactures a number of cast-iron grill pans which,
when used on the stove top, give meat, fish or vegetables
the taste of outdoor grilling. Some of the designs have
removable handles so that they can be easily transferred
from stove top to oven, and these handles can also be
folded for more convenient storage. Using traditional sand-
casting techniques, each piece is unique and takes a full
day to produce, but the result is some of the best cookware
money can buy.

Nambu Tekki saucepan, grill pan & mini brunch pan, 1999

Sori Yanagi (Japan, 1915–)

www.gatewayjapan.dk
Cast iron
Sori Yanagi, Valby, Denmark

Manufactured in Japan, the *Nambu Tekki* pans designed
by Sori Yanagi won a Japanese Good Design award in 2001.
Their subtle organic forms, with their slightly curved edges,
give the designs an enhanced functionality as well as a
distinctive beauty. Unlike normal cast iron, Japanese *nambu*
cast iron absorbs and distributes heat evenly, making it an
ideal material for cookware. Robust and durable, these pans
can be used on all kinds of heat sources.

Stainless steel pans & non-stick frying pans, 1990 & 1993

All-Clad Metalcrafters Design Team

www.all-clad.com
Stainless steel, aluminium, non-stick coating
All-Clad Metalcrafters, Canonsburg (PA), USA

All-Clad is held in high esteem across America thanks to the reputation of its premium cookware, which is made using a patented technology for bonding metal. The company's comprehensive *Stainless* range comprises numerous pots and pans of different shapes and sizes from which to make a selection. For example, these three-ply, bonded frying pans have highly durable, non-stick cooking surfaces and, as well as using them on a hob, they are also oven-safe up to 260°C (500°F).

Stainless pots & pans, 1990

All-Clad Metalcrafters Design Team

www.all-clad.com
Stainless steel, aluminium
All-Clad Metalcrafters, Canonsburg (PA), USA

America's bestselling premium cookware manufacturer, All-Clad is renowned for the impressive durability and cooking performance of its products. This *sauté* pan and matching saucepans have aluminium cores surrounded by three-ply, bonded stainless steel. This construction method ensures excellent heat distribution and responsive conduction of heat – put simply, they cook brilliantly. Handcrafted in the USA, All-Clad cookware comes with a lifetime warranty.

Copper-Core pots & pans, 1999

All-Clad Metalcrafters Design Team

www.all-clad.com
Stainless steel, copper
All-Clad Metalcrafters, Canonsburg (PA), USA

After years of research and development into the bonding of metals, John Ulam discovered that combining dissimilar metals could yield properties that they could never achieve individually. In 1971, he founded All-Clad Metalcrafters and began producing 'bonded' cookware for professional chefs using his patented processes. Today, the company produces a truly comprehensive range of stainless-steel pots and pans, with thick copper cores that distribute the heat evenly.

M'héritage casserole, sauté pan & saucepan, 1830 (original design)

Mauviel Design Team

www.mauviel.com
Copper, stainless steel, cast iron
Mauviel, Villedieu-les-Poêles, France

For centuries, copper pans have been used in the professional kitchens of France to create sublime gourmet food. Building on this tradition, the extensive *M'héritage* range of pots and pans – including this classic sauté pan, saucepan and casserole – combines the good heat conduction properties of traditional copper exteriors with the easy maintenance of modern stainless-steel interiors. Used by top chefs throughout the world, these archetypal cookware designs are available with cast-iron, bronze or stainless-steel handles.

Copper-Core seven-quart stockpot, c. 1999

All-Clad Metalcrafters Design Team

www.all-clad.com
Stainless steel, copper
All-Clad Metalcrafters, Canonsburg (PA), USA

All-Clad Metalcrafters' *Copper-Core* range of pots and pans are made from a unique five-ply, bonded construction of stainless steel and copper. The stainless steel is easy to clean and non-reactive, while the copper core gives optimum heat distribution. Handcrafted in America, the collection is sold with a lifetime guarantee, and includes: saucepans, *sauté* pans, a lidded Dutch oven, a *sauteuse, sauciers,* a buffet casserole, lidded casseroles, an open roaster, a butter warmer, a *cassoulet* and, shown here, the seven-quart (6.4-litre) stockpot.

Volcanic casserole, 1925

Le Creuset Design Team

www.lecreuset.com
Enamelled cast iron
Various sizes
Le Creuset, Fresnoy-le-Grand, France

Le Creuset's *Volcanic* collection is the quintessential range of French cast-iron pots and
pans. Unbelievably durable and superb for
slow cooking, the company's first, orange-
enamelled *cocotte* (casserole) was launched
in 1925. Since then, the range has grown and
new colours have been introduced. Even today,
after the pans have been cast, the majority of
the finishing is done by hand in order to give as
smooth a surface as possible for the subsequent high-fired enamelling.

Cocotte casserole, 1974

Francis Staub (France, active 1970s–2000s)

www.staub.fr
Enamelled cast iron, brass or stainless steel
0.25 l, 0.8 l, 1.4 l, 1.71 l, 2.24 l, 3.81 l, 4.6 l, 5.85 l, 8.35 l
Staub, Turckheim, France

The Staub company can trace its origins back to 1892, when a cookery store was opened in Alsace. However, it was not until 1974 that the founder's grandson, Francis Staub, purchased a nearby cast iron foundry and began manufacturing distinctive cooking pots to his own design. Unlike other, better-known cast-iron cookware, Staub pots and pans, such as these self-basting casseroles, have a matt-black enamel coating, which makes them virtually indestructible and highly resistant to chipping.

Tools cookware, 1998

Björn Dahlström (Sweden, 1957–)

www.iittala.com
Multi-layered stainless steel or cast iron
Iittala, Iittala, Finland

The *Tools* range is simply beautiful and superbly functional – in fact the fifteen pots and pans look so good, with their sturdy handles and satin-finished stainless steel or blackened cast-iron surfaces, that they can also be used to serve food. During their development, Dahlström worked with professional chefs and materials specialists to ensure that only the best and most appropriate materials according to potential use were utilized for each product.

Kokki casserole, 1978

Tapio Yli-Viikari (Finland, 1948–)

www.arabia.fi
Glazed ceramic
2.25 l, 3.25 l
Arabia/Iittala Group, Helsinki, Finland

As Director of the Ceramics and Glass Department at the University of Art and Design in Helsinki, Tapio Yli-Viikari understands both the aesthetic and manufacturing requirements of the ceramics industry. His wonderful *Kokki* casserole has been stripped of any extraneous detailing and, as such, possesses an ideal form guided by functional considerations. It is the three-dimensional realization of his belief that, 'Appropriateness is beauty'.

Sarpaneva cooking pot, 1960

Timo Sarpaneva (Finland, 1926–2006)

www.iittala.com
Enamelled cast iron, wood
3 l
Iittala, Iittala, Finland

Timo Sarpaneva's grandfather was a black-
smith, and as a child he spent time in his forge
watching ore magically turn into molten metal.
As an adult, this formative experience would
lead him to design a stylish and modern interpretation of the traditional, cast-iron cooking
pot. Although a basic and essential kitchen
item, Sarpaneva was able to bring innovation
to his design with a detachable wooden handle
that can be used to carry the pot, and also to
remove its lid when hot.

Pyrex lidded casserole, c. 1915 (original design)

Corning Design Team

www.pyrex.com
Pyrex®
0.75 l, 1.25 l, 2 l
Corning, Corning (NY), USA

Pyrex® is a type of borosilicate glass that can withstand temperatures up to 300°C (572°F). It is also microwave, freezer and dishwasher safe, and stain resistant – making it a highly versatile material for cookware. Easily indentified by its clean lines and slight azure tint, *Pyrex* cookware, such as this classic lidded casserole, is exceptionally functional, eminently affordable and extremely durable.

Pyrex bakeware, c. 1915 (original design)

Corning Design Team

www.pyrex.com
Pyrex®
Various sizes
Corning, Corning (NY), USA

Pyrex bakeware is such a ubiquitous item in so many homes that we have come to take it for granted, and tend to overlook its many attributes. Designed from a completely rational aspect and honed over decades, these classic designs are superbly adapted to their roles. Impressively robust and democratically inexpensive, with proper care they should last a lifetime.

M'cook roasting pan, 2003

Mauviel Design Team

www.mauviel.com
Stainless steel, aluminium
↕ 7 cm ↔ 35 cm ⤢ 25 cm
↕ 8.5 cm ↔ 40 cm ⤢ 30 cm
Mauviel, Villedieu-les-Poêles, France

This sturdy, stainless-steel roasting pan has an aluminium core that provides excellent heat conductivity which, in turn, means an even cooking temperature and better perform-ance all round. Designed to last a lifetime, the roaster has large handles that are easy to grip when using oven mitts. It is made to exacting and traditionally artisanal standards by Mauviel, a French company based near Mont Saint Michel that has specialized in the produc-tion of superlative cookware since 1830.

Sancerre baking/roasting dishes, 1986

Michel Roux (France, 1951–)

www.pillivuyt.fr
Fireproof hardened china
↔ 44.5, 37.5 cm
Pillivuyt, Mehun-sur-Yèvre, France

Established in 1818, Pillivuyt is one of the
leading producers of fine white porcelain in
France. The simplicity of its ceramic forms and
the absence of any colour or decoration ensure
that food is shown to its best advantage – a
blank canvas on which the art of fine cuisine
can be displayed. These heat-resistant dishes
can be used for baking as well as serving, and
stack efficiently for storage.

Oval stackable dishes, 1999

Francis Staub (France, active 1970s–2000s)

www.staub.fr
Enamelled cast iron
↔ 15, 21, 24, 28, 32 cm
Staub, Turckheim, France

Admired by many celebrated world-class chefs, Staub cookware is not only highly durable but also enables good heat distribution and retention, thereby enhancing the flavours of what is being prepared. Every piece of cookware produced by the company has been personally designed by its founder, Francis Staub, and is individually produced in a sand mould, which is destroyed after each casting. These restaurant-quality roasting dishes are perfect for cooking a wide array of foods, and nest into one another for efficient storage.

L25W3-3630 wok, 1992 (original design)

Le Creuset Design Team

www.lecreuset.com
Enamelled metal, heat-resistant glass, plastic
⌀ 36 cm
Le Creuset, Fresnoy-le-Grand, France

Part of Le Creuset's *International Range*, this elegant wok was designed specifically for oriental cooking and has a flat base for maximum heat efficiency and stability. Unlike traditional round-based woks, this design is suitable for all types of hobs and is also oven, grill, freezer and dishwasher safe. It can also be used for steaming, poaching and braising, and comes with a handy see-through, heat-resistant cover. The *L25W3-3630* is available in orange, blue, red, grey and black.

Stainless steamer set, 1990s

All-Clad Metalcrafters Design Team

www.all-clad.com
Stainless steel
11.35 l
All-Clad Metalcrafters, Canonsburg (PA), USA

Probably the best steamer money can buy, this versatile All-Clad design is extremely durable and, according to the testimonies of users, it performs exceptionally well. Perfect for steaming vegetables when used with its steamer insert, this sturdy pan can also be used by itself as a traditional saucepan. All-Clad also manufactures a smaller, 2.5-quart (2.3-litre) version, which is the perfect size for smaller families.

Good Grips pop-up steamer, 2006

Bally Design (USA, est. 1972)

www.oxo.com
Stainless steel, Santoprene
⌀ 17.8 cm
OXO International, New York (NY), USA

Although there has been a trend
in recent years to use electric
steamers, they actually take up
a lot of cupboard space when not
in use, and their cooking results
can be a bit haphazard – vegetables often seem more stewed
than steamed. Instead, this
simple pop-up steamer is not only
compact for storage, but also gives
excellent cooking results: less is
sometimes more.

Springform bakeware, 1919

Wilhelm Ferdinand Kaiser (Germany, active 1910s)

www.kaiserbakeware.com
Stainless steel
Various sizes
WF Kaiser, Diez, Germany

In 1919, Wilhelm Ferdinand Kaiser began manufacturing a small range of European-style bakeware items that incorporated his new 'springform' invention, which allowed the easy release of baked cakes or tortes. Today, the business he founded produces over thirty different *Springform* pans, all of which are manufactured with steel bases. This, in the words of the company, 'provides even and gentle heat distribution for the even browning and baking generally found in professional kitchens … so you can produce a perfectly moist, tender cake'.

Original Zeroll ice-cream scoop, 1933

Sherman Kelly (USA, 1869–1952)

www.zeroll.com
Aluminium alloy
↕ 18 cm
Zeroll, Fort Pierce (FL), USA

Simply the best ice-cream scoop in the world, Zeroll's classic design has been in continuous production for more than seventy years. Designed by the inventor Sherman L Kelly, it uses a heat-conductive liquid in the handle which, when warmed by the hand, assists the bowl to release even the hardest ice cream. Its superior performance and indestructibility make it the scoop of choice in ice-cream parlours across America.

AJ Cylinda Line ice bucket & tongs, 1967

Arne Jacobsen (Denmark, 1902–1971)

www.stelton.com
Stainless steel
1 l, 2.5 l
Stelton, Copenhagen, Denmark

Epitomizing the effortless sophistication of Danish
Modernism, Arne Jacobsen's ice bucket and matching tongs
are made from high-grade, satin-polished stainless steel,
and the former comes in two sizes: one litre and 2.5 litres.
As part of Stelton's well-known *AJ Cylinda Line*, the ice
bucket and tongs perfectly compliment other designs from
the range, including a serving tray and a revolving ashtray.

16850 trivets, 1997

Rösle Design Team

www.roesle.de
Stainless steel, silicone
⌀ 12, 18, 25 cm
Rösle, Marktoberdorf, Germany

Rösle's trivets fit into each other for compact storage, and can either be used individually as separate rings or together, in which configuration they resemble a target. Each of the three circular trivets has silicone feet to protect the surface underneath from heat or scratching. Like other Rösle products, these useful designs are also beautiful objects in their own right, and will enhance any kitchen.

Dé(s)licieux cake knife, 2006

Matali Crasset (France, 1965–) & Pierre Hermé (France, 1961–)

www.forge-de-laguiole.com
Stainless steel, silicone
Forge de Laguiole, Laguiole, France

Since the late 1980s, the Forge de Laguiole has commissioned various leading French designers to create superior contemporary tools for living. In 2006, Matali Crasset collaborated with the famous Parisian pastry chef, Pierre Hermé, to create the innovative *Dé(s)licieux* cake knife. This exquisite kitchen implement not only slices *les gateaux* perfectly, but serves them up rather wonderfully too. Comfortable to hold with its softly contoured two-tone handle, this cake knife is also an object of beauty in its own right.

Astoria kitchen cart, 2005

Enrico Albertini (Italy, 1971–)

www.legnoart.it
Solid wood, stainless steel
↕ 92 cm ↔ 80 cm ↗ 60 cm
Legnoart, Omegna, Italy

Located near Lake Orta, some 50 miles outside Milan, Legnoart is a family business run by Enrico Albertini, who is also the company's chief designer. The original version of this trolley won the coveted Prix de la Découverte at the Maison & Objet exhibition in Paris a decade ago, but was restyled in 2005. This new version boasts a sturdy solid wooden frame, an end-grain worktop, six drawers, a stainless-steel lift-out bin, bottle holders, tool hangers and wheels with stabilizing brakes.

A classic design that has stood the test of time, the *Le Parfait Super* jar debuted in the 1930s and has changed little over the succeeding years. Durably robust and stylishly utilitarian, 'the perfect' domestic canning jar (as its title translates), with its distinctive orange rubber seal, comes in a range of sizes and can be reused over the years for the preserving of vegetables, fruits and more. Practical and inexpensive, this seminal French design is now gaining popularity as more people rediscover the healthful joys of home canning – today more than twenty million units are sold *per annum*, a fifty per cent increase in ten years.

Le Parfait Super jars, 1930s

Le Parfait Design Team

www.leparfait.com
Glass, metal, rubber
0.5, 0.75, 1, 1.5, 2, 3 l
Le Parfait, Reims, France

Storage kitchen containers, 2002

Bodum Design Group

www.bodum.com
Borosilicate glass, oiled beech, silicone
0.6 l, 1 l, 1.9 l, 2 l, 2.5 l
Bodum, Triengen, Switzerland

Widely used for laboratory wares, borosilicate glass is also an ideal material for storage containers because it is both inert and resistant to heat, water, acids and salt solutions. These inherent properties ensure that it cannot taint any foodstuffs with which it comes into contact. Bodum's storage vessels are also made from a special type of borosilicate glass that contains no lead and has a distinctive brilliance. These functional and durable containers are topped off with oiled beech lids and silicone gaskets to provide an airtight seal.

Endurance saltcellar with spoon, 2007

RSVP International Design Team

www.rsvp-intl.com
Stainless steel, glass, silicone
0.23 l
RSVP International, Seattle (WA), USA

Intended for both the kitchen and the dining table, the *Endurance* saltcellar can be used to store gourmet sea salt, which is now available in a startling array of colours and flavours, from pink Himalayan salt to Hawaiian black salt. Its flip-top lid has a silicone gasket that protects the salt crystals from atmospheric moisture, thereby keeping them fresh and dry. Dishwasher proof, the salt cellar's glass bowl holds up to eight ounces of salt (almost a standard cup measure).

Roll Top bread bin, 2007

Brabantia Design Team

www.brabantia.com
Galfan-coated stainless steel, plastic
↕ 18.9 cm ↔ 47.9 cm ↗ 27.6 cm
Brabantia, Emmerlich, Germany

Widely available and extremely popular, this bread bin has a variety of useful features. Although relatively compact, it has a two-loaf capacity and, thanks to its roll-top door, it doesn't take up too much space on the work surface. It also has a corrosion-resistant coating, a knobbly patterned base for correct ventilation and a plastic noise-dampening stop. Backed up by a ten-year guarantee, this classic German-made design is a no-frills tool that does its job with great efficiency and functional durability.

Mary Biscuit container, 1995

Stefano Giovannoni (Italy 1954–)

www.alessi.com
EVA, PMMA
↕ 11.5 cm   ↔ 28 cm   ↗ 22 cm
Alessi, Milan, Italy

Stefano Giovannoni will often use metaphor
in his playful approach to design. In the
Mary Biscuit container, the biscuit-shaped
lid symbolises the overall concept, while
the actual container provides useful airtight
storage for cookies. The resulting design is not
only functional but emotionally seductive, and
makes reaching for the cookies as delightful as
eating them.

CamSquares storage containers, 1960s (original design)

Cambro Design Team

www.cambro.com
Polycarbonate, polyethylene
2–22 quarts (1.89–20.8 l)
Cambro Manufacturing Company,
Huntington Beach (CA), USA

In 1951, Bill Campbell invented the *Camtray* (a plastic canteen tray) and, along with his brother, founded a company to produce and market his innovative and ubiquitous design to the 'food-service' sector. Later, the Cambro company launched the world's first transparent plastic food container, which has now evolved into the extensive *CamSquares* stackable storage range, with its snap-tight, colour-coded lids and crystal clear or translucent white polycarbonate bodies. Astonishingly, these products can withstand temperatures ranging from −40 °C to 99 °C (104 °F to 210 °F).

Elemaris XL Chrome water filter jug, 2005

Brita Design Team

www.brita.co.uk
Plastic, non-slip rubber
2.2 l
Brita, Taunusstein, Germany

Founded in 1966, Brita has been a leader in water filtration or as it puts it 'water optimization' for more than forty years. In 1970, it launched its first water filter jug for domestic use, and has since honed this design to incorporate the latest technologies. Today, its top-of-the-line *Elemaris XL Chrome* water filter jug has an electronic cartridge exchange indicator, an ergonomic soft grip, a non-slip rubber base and an easy-to-fill, pour-through lid.

Morrison Toaster, 2004

Jasper Morrison (UK, 1959–)

www.rowenta.com
Polypropylene, steel
↔ 25.5 cm
Rowenta Werke, Offenbach am Main, Germany

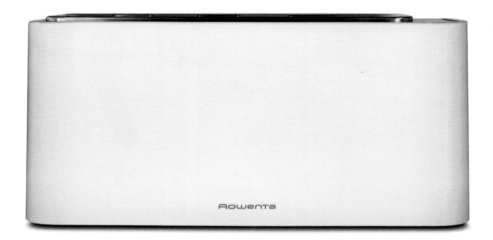

Like other kitchen appliances designed by
Jasper Morrison for Rowenta, this toaster is a
functionally and aesthetically unified design
that is both elegant and timeless. Integrated
into its clean white housing are a wide range
of innovative features, from a photo-sensor
browning control and a soft-eject crumb tray,
to an LED display and audible signal. As a pure
and essentialist design, the *Morrison Toaster*
is reminiscent of the landmark kitchenware
designed for Braun in the 1960s by Dieter Rams.

Morrison Kettle, 2004

Jasper Morrison (UK, 1959–)

www.rowenta.com
Polypropylene, steel
1.5 l
Rowenta Werke, Offenbach am Main, Germany

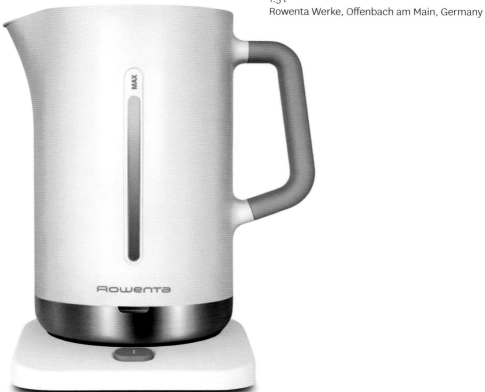

This cordless electric kettle not only looks good, but also has a powerful and smoothly polished stainless-steel element that combats scaling and provides rapid heating. Like other designs by Morrison, this kettle contains numerous indications of his careful and considered approach, for instance: a removable lid for easy cleaning (which also incorporates a scale-trapping filter), and a base that can be used to store the excess cord. A functional and essentialist design, the *Morrison Kettle* received the Chicago Athenaeum's Good Design Award in 2004.

Braun Impression HT 600 toaster, 2003

Björn Kling (Germany, 1965–)

www.braun.com
Various materials
↔ 43 cm
Braun, Kronberg, Germany

Acknowledging that contemporary kitchens are frequently used as living spaces as well as for cooking, Braun's design team created the *Impression Line*. Their guiding principle was that kitchen equipment, such as this long-slotted toaster, should perform its tasks perfectly while also being intrinsically beautiful. As one of Braun's in-house designers, Björn Kling, notes: 'Everyday living should be simple to master – with simplicity that's not only functional, but beautiful. This is the Braun philosophy'.

Braun Impression WK 600 kettle, 2003

Björn Kling (Germany, 1965–)

www.braun.com
Various materials
1.7 l
Braun, Kronberg, Germany

Björn Kling's *Impression Line,*
including the kettle shown here,
raises the aesthetic level of kitchen
equipment and reflects his desire
to enhance daily life through
beautiful design. Although a simple
concept, this is sadly one all too
often forgotten in the realm of
kitchen products. This kettle, with
its easy-filling spout and easily
readable water level indicator,
demonstrates that even the
simplest everyday object can be
imbued with a sense of style.

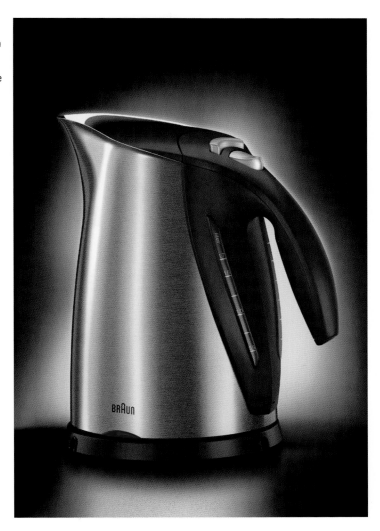

Combi 2×2 toaster, 1948

Max Gore-Barten (UK, 1914–)

www.dualit.com
Chromed stainless steel
↔ 36 cm
Dualit, Crawley, UK

Originally designed for use in commercial kitchens, Dualit's iconic toasters have an endearing, no-nonsense robustness, which makes them incredibly durable. The retro *Combi* incorporates patented and award-winning ProHeat elements, and has a simple mechanical timer to control toasting time. In order to ensure the highest manufacturing quality, the design is still hand-built by the company founded by Max Gore-Barten in 1945.

TW911P2 kettle, 1997

Porsche Design Studio (Austria, est. 1972)

www.siemens-homeappliances.com
Brushed aluminium, other materials
↕ 27.7 cm
Siemens, Munich, Germany

Manufactured by Siemens, the *Porsche Design Collection* has raised the aesthetic and functional bar of home appliances to a new level. Winning a prestigious iF design award in 2006, the collection's 1.5-litre cordless kettle has a thermally insulated, cool-touch body that incorporates a double-sided water level indicator. A brushed aluminium and black plastic polymer exterior lend style to the design, while its precise engineering alludes to the excellence of Germany's automotive heritage.

Nespresso Siemens TK911N2GB coffee maker, 2005

Porsche Design Studio (Austria, est. 1972)

www.nespresso.com
Brushed aluminum, PMMA
↕ 34.7 cm
Siemens, Munich, Germany/Nestlé Nespresso, Paudex, Switzerland

This elegant and high-tech design incorporates the
Nespresso coffee-making system, which employs easy-
to-use disposable capsules. Apart from making espressos,
this is the first machine of its kind to have a one-touch function to create cappuccinos or café lattes as well. The design
also incorporates a special frothing nozzle and cup-warming
plate. Using an engineering approach, Porsche Design
creates products that are distinguished by a remarkable
level of purity and precision.

Essenza c90 coffee maker, 2003

Antoine Cahen (Switzerland, 1950–) & Philippe
Cahen (Switzerland, 1947–)

www.nespresso.com
ABS, PMMA, stainless steel
↕ 29.1 cm
Nestlé Nespresso, Paudex, Switzerland

Since 1988, the Swiss brothers Antoine and Philippe Cahen
have designed nine coffee-making machines for Nestlé
Nespresso. Their *Essenza* machine, which won a Red Dot
Best of the Best award in 2005, is a compact machine
intended for a wide range of consumers with smaller
kitchens, from students to condo owners and the retired.
Developed in conjunction with Nespresso's engineers, this
machine was designed around a new extraction system
through which a smaller and more unified design was
achieved.

Francis Francis X1 espresso machine, 1995

Luca Trazzi (Italy, 1962–)

www.illy.com
Steel, brass, plastic, bronze
↕ 30 cm
Illy, Trieste, Italy

In 1935, Francesco Illy designed the first automatic espresso machine, known as the *Illetta*, which used compressed air to force steam through coffee grounds. Like its predecessor, the *Francis Francis X1* home espresso machine also makes superlative coffee, while its unusual styling has been described by *Wired* magazine as 'retro-futuristic'. Designed by the Italian architect Luca Trazzi, this eighteen-bar, pump-driven espresso machine has a strong aesthetic presence.

Morrison Coffee Machine, 2004

Jasper Morrison (UK, 1959–)

www.rowenta.com
Polypropylene, steel, glass
↕ 37.6 cm
Rowenta Werke, Offenbach am Main, Germany

This 'all-in-one' coffee machine has been designed from a purely functional aspect, with its minimalist and Modernist aesthetic following directly from Jasper Morrison's essentialist approach to design. The removable filter holder, coffee measure and filter papers are concealed in the top section. The glass or thermal jugs, however, are integrated into the machine's main body, ensuring a very clean and discreet appearance. The design also incorporates a 'pause-and-serve' feature, and will turn itself off automatically after two hours.

Squeeze citrus press & jug, 1999

Hendrik Holbaek (Denmark, 1960–) & Claus Jensen (Denmark, 1966–)

www.evasolo.com
Glass, stainless steel, plastic
0.6 l
Eva Solo, Maaloev, Denmark

Comprising just three elements – a glass jug, a plastic funnel and a star-shaped dome of polished stainless steel – the *Squeeze* is an elegant and effective citrus-pressing solution. Requiring virtually no force, the juice flows from the cut fruit into the funnel, which filters out any pips, and then pulp-rich juice collects in the jug for immediate serving. This dishwasher-safe design received a Formland award in 1999 and an iF design award in 2002.

Better known for its toasted sandwich makers, Breville also manufactures the *Juice Fountain Elite* – a commercial-grade juicer designed specifically for the high-end domestic user. Before its launch in 1999, no juicer could process whole apples or pears, and an eight ounce glass of juice took on average more than three minutes to extract. In comparison, the revolutionary *Juice Fountain* takes only five seconds. The reason for this is that its feed tube is placed directly above the center of the cutting disc; and it also incorporates patented, dual-action, stabilizing blades that grind the pulp into smaller particles, thereby producing a higher juice-to-fruit yield.

Juice Fountain Elite 800 JEXL juice extractor, 1999

Breville Design Team

www.breville.com
Die-cast aluminium, zinc, stainless steel
↕ 40.6 cm
Breville, Sydney, Australia

Model MBB520 food & beverage blender, 1998

Waring Design Team

www.waringproducts.com
Metal, plastic, glass
1.18 l
Waring, Torrington (CT), USA

Waring introduced the first blender, known as the *Miracle Mixer* to the American public in 1937. It was designed by Fred Osius, who believed his new invention would 'revolutionize people's eating habits', which it certainly did. Since then, the company has become a well-respected manufacturer of high-quality and durable blenders, including the *Waring Pro MBB Series*. With its trademark cloverleaf glass carafe, heavy-duty metal base and simple two-speed operation, the *Model MBB520* is actually based on an earlier design from 1948 by Peter Muller-Munk.

Bamix Gastro 350 hand blender, 2007

Bamix Design Team

www.bamix.com
Various materials
↕ 49.5 cm
Bamix of Switzerland, Mettlen, Switzerland

In the early 1950s, Roger Perrinjaquet invented the first wand mixer, which was christened the *Bamix*, a catchy abbreviation of the French *'battre et mixer'* ('beat and mix'). Since then, more than seven million of these high-quality and impressively robust hand blenders have been manufactured, each incorporating a virtually indestructible motor that was specially designed for this product. The most recent version, the *Gastro 350* has two speeds and a comfortable soft grip. It is also corrosion-resistant, odour-resistant and, most importantly, taste-resistant, making it the firm favourite of professional chefs.

kMix stand mixer, 2007

Youmeus (UK, est. 2003)

www.kenwoodworld.com
Aluminium, stainless steel
↕ 34.9 cm ↔ 36.1 cm ↗ 22.3 cm
Kenwood, Havant, UK

In 1948 the first *Kenwood Chef* mixer was launched and immediately became a much-loved labour-saving feature in kitchens across Britain. Twelve years later, a redesigned model by Kenneth Grange was introduced and went on to achieve British 'design icon' status. Against this impressive heritage, Youmeus were tasked to create a new food mixer that brought the values of the well-known brand into the 21st century. The resulting *kMix* is not only visually stunning but also extremely functional.

Artisan KSM150 kitchen stand mixer, 1937

Egmont Arens (USA, 1888–1966)

www.kitchenaid.com
Polished stainless steel, other materials
↕ 35.8 cm
KitchenAid, St Joseph (MI), USA

Like other industrial designers who gained prominence in America during the 1930s, Arens was engaged by manufacturers to make their products more alluring to consumers through bold, streamlined styling. His classic mixer for KitchenAid, originally known as the *Model K,* is his best-known design, and it is a tribute to his work that it has remained in production, virtually unaltered, for over seventy years. A true icon of American design, this retro design is a robustly functional yet eye-catching addition to any kitchen.

Good Grips Stainless Steel soap dispenser, 2005

Smart Design (USA, est. 1978)

www.oxo.com
Stainless steel, polycarbonate
↕ 22.7 cm
OXO International, New York (NY), USA

Good soap dispensers for the kitchen are difficult to find – most work well for a short while and then start to drip annoyingly. Produced by OXO, this elegant design promises to be different, with an easy-to-dispense mechanism that is ideal for people with age-related dexterity problems. Its non-slip top button allows liquid soap or washing-up liquid to be squirted without difficulty, while the non-slip base ensures stability and the wide-mouthed screw top makes it simple to refill.

Quick Load paper towel holder, 2004

Simplehuman Design Team & Lum Design Associates (USA, est. 1999)

www.simplehuman.com
Stainless steel, plastic
Simplehuman, Torrance (CA), USA

Every kitchen needs one, but most paper towel holders are less than well designed. Simplehuman's answer to this problem is, of course, a product with features that make it easier to use. The *Quick Load* is made from sturdy stainless steel, making it more stable when tearing off a sheet of kitchen roll. It also has a grooved edge along its base to stop the nuisance of unravelling paper, while its quick-release knob permits speedy roll changing.

SteeL palm brush, 2007

Smart Design (USA, est. 1978)

www.oxo.com
Steel, Santoprene, nylon
oxo International, New York (NY), USA

One of the most recent additions to the oxo range, the *SteeL* palm brush is meant for dish cleaning, and like other products in the collection has a soft, non-slip grip. Its durable nylon bristles are stiff enough to scrub and scour away baked-on food, yet soft enough to use on non-stick cookware without fear of scratching. Like other products designed by Smart Design for oxo, this handy little brush can be used by all ages thanks to its 'inclusive' ergonomic design.

Long-Handled Cleaning Brush, 2004

Cuisipro Design Team

www.cuisipro.com
Stainless steel, ABS, nylon
Cuisipro, Markham, Ontario, Canada

This ergonomic cleaning brush promises to make light work of dirty dishes, pots and pans. The reservoir of washing-up liquid can be seen inside the handle, and is dispensed though its leak-proof cleaning head using a pump-action mechanism. Three different, interchangeable heads are available: bristle, scrubbing sponge and soft sponge. Made to last with its durable stainless-steel handle, this is a useful yet attractive addition to any kitchen.

Dish Doctor dish rack, 1997

Marc Newson (Australia, 1963–)

www.magisdesign.com
Injection-moulded glossy polypropylene
Magis, Motta di Livenza, Italy

Marc Newson's dish rack is an innovative and playful
solution that has enlivened many a kitchen with its bright
colours and unusual form. It has an integral drainer and
comes in two pieces so that the collected water can easily
be poured away. Alternatively, you can just use the top
section on an existing draining board. Funky and futuristic
the *Dish Doctor* was an instant success when launched,
thanks to the ability of Magis to mould polypropylene so
that the surface finish literally glistens.

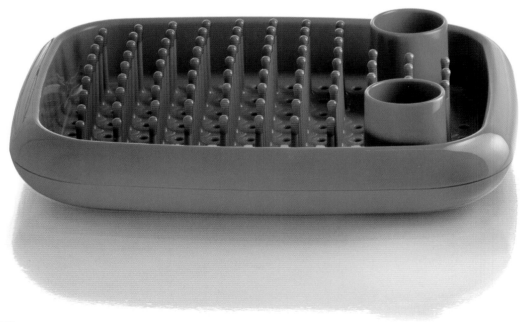

Steel Frame dish rack, 2007

Simplehuman Design Team & Lum Design Associates (USA, est. 1999)

www.simplehuman.com
Coated stainless steel, bamboo, plastic
Simplehuman, Torrance (CA), USA

With extra rungs that can be flipped up when required, and a sliding section for holding cups, this dish rack is a highly space-efficient design that can be adapted according to how many glasses, plates, pots or pans need to be drained. There is also a bamboo knife block to protect knives as they dry. In addition, the rack has been treated with a finger-proof and smudge-resistant coating so that the stainless steel will remain gleaming.

Aga Classic Special Edition 4 heat storage cooker, 1930s

Gustaf Dalén (Sweden, 1869–1937)

www.aga-rayburn.co.uk
Cast iron, other materials
↔ 148.7 cm
Aga, Telford, UK

Using the concept of heat storage, the Nobel Prize-winning physicist, Gustaf Dalén, invented the *Aga* cooker in the late 1920s. Incorporating a small but highly efficient heat source, *Aga* cookers have various ovens and hotplates that maintain different temperatures. They can, therefore, be used for different types of cooking, from roasting and grilling to frying and steaming. A veritable icon of durable domestic design, this special edition model is based on an original *Aga* cooker from the 1930s and incorporates four ovens.

Professional Series range, 1987 (original design)

Viking Design Team

www.vikingrange.com
Stainless steel, glass, other materials
↔ 121.6 cm
Viking, Greenwood (MS), USA

During the 1970s, a building contractor by the name of
Fred Carl Jr noticed that commercial cooking ranges were
increasingly being specified for domestic interiors. Their
industrial look was, it seemed, in tune with the then fash-
ionable High Tech style. As a result, Carl founded the Viking
Range Corporation in the early 1980s to manufacture hybrid,
heavy-duty ranges that gave the performance of professional equipment but that were also tailored to the home.
Today, Viking manufactures a range of premium equipment
suitable for furnishing any chef's dream kitchen.

Professional Series combi-steam oven, 2007

Viking Design Team

www.vikingrange.com
Stainless steel, glass, other materials
↔ 59.4 cm
Viking, Greenwood (MS), USA

By using a combination of steam and convection heat, this oven provides a fast and healthy way of cooking. As you would expect from Viking, the design boasts numerous professional features, including six different cooking functions – such as the ReHeat Plus option that reheats and defrosts foods using steam. In addition, the design has an automatic de-scaling and cleaning feature.

Professional Series microwave, 2002

Viking Design Team

www.vikingrange.com
Stainless steel, glass, other materials
↔ 62.5 cm
Viking, Greenwood (MS), USA

Like other premium kitchen equipment manufactured by
Viking, the *Professional Series* microware provides performance far beyond the domestic norm with its extra-large
capacity and its array of broiling, roasting and baking
settings, alongside conventional microwave functions.
In a multitude of ways, it will cook or re-heat your food
to perfection. Apart from the stainless-steel version, this
design comes in twenty-three different colour options,
and can either be placed on a counter top or installed as a
built-in unit.

P775-1 ceramic hob, 2001–2002

Smeg Design Team

www.smeg.com
Ceramic, stainless steel
↔ 60, 72 cm
Smeg, Guastella, Italy

Smeg's motto, 'technology with style', perfectly describes the company's understated yet high-quality kitchen appliances. Engineering excellence, combined with a human-centric approach to design, ensures that Smeg equipment – such as the *P775-1* ceramic hob – has a logical and functional elegance that is impervious to the vagaries of fashions. The *P775-1's* five cooking zones are controlled using the firm's exclusive 'rocker touch control', that provides nine different power levels and an independent time-programming facility.

P75 hob, 2005

Piano Design (Italy, est. 1981)

www.smeg.com
Stainless steel
↔ 72 cm
Smeg, Guastella, Italy

This hob is one of three models designed by Piano Design for Smeg. Like Renzo Piano's architecture, this sleek design – with its harmonious proportions, uncluttered lines and refined detailing (such as the visually stunning pan stands) – can be seen as an elegant expression of post-Miesian Modern Neo-Classicism. In addition, the hob's five burners have safety valves that automatically shut off the gas supply if the flame is accidentally extinguished.

Professional Series chimney wall hood, 2007 & Professional Series island hood, 2003

Viking Design Team

www.vikingrange.com
Stainless steel
↔ 75.9, 91.1, 106.4, 121.6, 136.8, 152.1, 167.3 cm
Viking, Greenwood (MS), USA

The heavy-duty construction of these professional-style chimney hoods is virtually seamless, with no visible screws. This underwrites their super-stylish looks, and also ensures that it is easier to keep them clean and gleaming. These hoods also outperform most other designs currently on the market thanks to a commercial-standard baffle filter system that quickly and efficiently removes grease and heated vapours from the air.

J-series refrigerator, 2007

Jasper Morrison (UK, 1959–)

www.samsung.com
Various materials
↔ 91.2 cm
Samsung, Seoul, Korea

As Jasper Morrison explains, 'Design has taken a foothold in the modern home and appliances now need to exceed customer expectations and offer users an emotional experience.' Certainly, his side-by-side *J-series* refrigerator for Samsung, which took two years to develop, manages harmoniously to synthesize state-of-the-art technology with a pure and modern look. Happily, the resulting design not only offers high functional performance and good energy efficiency, but also has an engaging yet minimalist aesthetic.

B1-48S refrigerator/freezer, 2010

Sub-Zero Design Team

www.subzero.com
Various materials
↔ 121.9 cm
Sub-Zero Freezer Company, Madison (WI), USA

Often regarded as the king of cool, Sub-Zero was the first company to introduce built-in home refrigerators in the mid-1950s. Since then, the company has continually refined its concept, and today produces premium, American-style refrigerators that symbolise that nation's alluring vision of scale and plenty. This side-by-side fridge-freezer, fully clad in stainless steel, is one of the company's most stylish models, and boasts an impressive 276.7 litre capacity.

Blanco Claron 8S-IF sink, 2006

Blanco Design Team

www.blanco.de
Stainless steel
↔ 116 cm
Blanco, Oberderdingen, Germany

The *Blanco Claron 8s-IF* double-bowl sink is a premier solution that can be inset into a counter-top or flush mounted.
Made of satin-polished stainless steel, this elegantly
practical sink has an engineered purity that has become
synonymous with the best of modern German design. This
revolutionary design has won both a Red Dot design award
and an iF product design award, not least for its beautiful
and distinctive contours, which prescribe a precise and
seamless transition from curves into straight lines.

Kitchen unit (VSR 70 sink, A 478/4G countertop hob, TS/190 counter top, 2CL/190 drawers & cabinet), c. 2008

Nico Moretto (Italy, 1926–)

www.alpesinox.com
Stainless steel
↔ 190 cm
Alpes-Inox, Bassano del Grappa, Italy

Winner of a Compasso d'Oro, Nico Moretto has developed an outstanding and truly comprehensive range of kitchen units made up of modular, moveable and independent elements that can be arranged and configured according to need and available space. The design of these units, such as the one shown here, are determined by careful ergonomic study, while their manufacture relies on skilled craftsmen working with the finest grade of stainless steel.

Artematica modular kitchen, 1988

Valcucine Design Team

www.valcucine.it
Aluminium, lacquered MDF, glass, laminates
Valcucine, Pordenone, Italy

Valcucine specializes in the manufacture of environmentally friendly modular kitchens. Their production involves
a minimum of materials and energy; they are made from
recyclable components and sustainably sourced woods;
and the company's manufacturing process reduces toxic
and polluting chemical emissions. Valcucine's products are
also designed to be as durable as possible to ensure their
longevity. In addition, their *Artematica* kitchen is extremely
functional and elegant, showing that eco-sustainable design
can also be exceedingly stylish.

Kitchen 1, 2005

Jacob Jensen (Denmark, 1926–)
& Timothy Jacob Jensen (Denmark 1962–)

www.lifa-design.com
Teak or maple, aluminium, laminate
↗ 90 cm
Lifa Design, Holstebro, Denmark

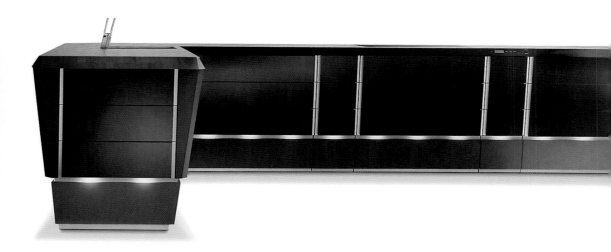

Jacob Jensen is known for his seminal audio-equipment designs for Bang & Olufsen and his eponymous homeware collection, which ranges from alarm clocks to doorbells. With his son Timothy, he has more recently turned his attention to designing on a larger scale. The resulting *Kitchen 1* and *Kitchen 2* were inspired by the landscape of Northern Denmark where the Jensen design studio is located – the surrounding scenery described by Timothy as "pure lines, simple forms, contrasts of light and dark."

Kitchen 2, 2007

Jacob Jensen (Denmark, 1926–)
& Timothy Jacob Jensen (Denmark 1962–)

www.lifa-design.com
Laminate, oak, teak or maple
↗ 90 cm
Lifa Design, Holstebro, Denmark

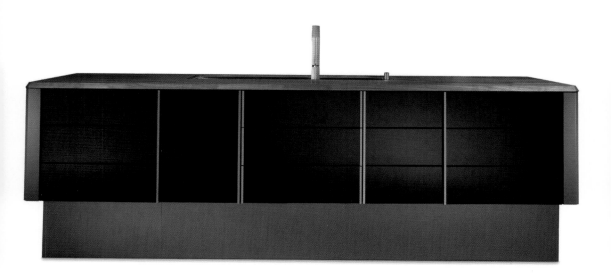

According to their manufacturer, *Kitchen 1* and *Kitchen 2* are 'the kitchen industry's answer to Formula 1'. The concept behind them is to create a timeless solution that relies on dynamic, faceted forms and simple bold lines. Both kitchens possess a functional purity and, like other Jensen designs, have an extraordinarily high level of build quality. Designed without compromise, these kitchens are available in just two finishes: white or black.

Bulthaup b1 Kitchen System, 2008

Bulthaup Design Team

www.bulthaup.com
Veneered or lacquered MDF
Bulthaup, Bodenkirchen, Germany

Marketed as the 'essential kitchen', the *Bulthaup b1* is a
system of kitchen units with a timelessly beautiful, pared-
down aesthetic. Inspired by ideas of 'simplicity, geometry,
sensuality', the precision-manufactured modular elements
are made from basic cuboid shapes, and can be flexibly
combined to suit individual requirements. Thanks to its
restrained and essentialist look, the *Bulthaup b1* fits well
into any architectural setting.

Blackhandle cutlery, 1982

Sori Yanagi (Japan, 1915–)

www.soriyanagi.com
Stainless steel, lacquered compressed betula wood
Sori Yanagi, Valby, Denmark

An exquisite expression of Japanese simplicity and functionality, Sori Yanagi's *Blackhandle* cutlery range is manufactured in the Niigata region of Japan, long famed for its traditional metalworking craftsmanship and the superlative quality of its steel. The lacquered handles are made of compressed betula wood (Japanese birch) and have a pleasurable feel when dining. Quite simply, this cutlery range is a superb example of Japanese design that can be used every day.

Steel cutlery, 1974

Sori Yanagi (Japan, 1915–)

www.soriyanagi.com
Stainless steel
Sori Yanagi, Valby, Denmark

For centuries, Japan's Niigata prefecture has been famed for its tableware, a reputation founded, in turn, on the region's outstanding craftsmanship and the quality of its steel. Sori Yanagi's *Steel* cutlery range, manufactured by skilled craftsmen from this area, is beautifully made and possesses a high degree of functionality, expressed through its clean modern lines. Dishwasher safe, this cutlery won a Japanese Good Design award in 1974, and also a Long Life award in 2001.

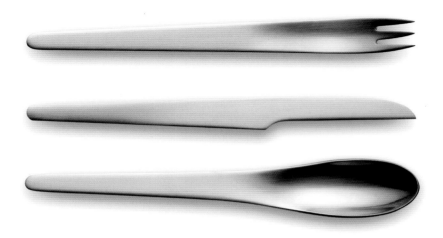

AJ cutlery, 1957

Arne Jacobsen (Denmark, 1902–1971)

www.georgjensen.com
Stainless steel
Georg Jensen, Copenhagen, Denmark

Arne Jacobsen originally designed the well-known AJ cutlery range as part of his unified scheme for the SAS Royal Hotel in Copenhagen, which is widely acknowledged as an architectural masterwork of the International Style. Minimal and elegant, the cutlery, which sits comfortably in the hand, must have seemed strikingly futuristic when first launched. In production for over fifty years, it has come to be known as 'cutlery without frills', and still retains a strong sense of contemporary stylishness.

Duna cutlery, 1995

Marco Zanuso (Italy, 1916–2001)

www.alessi.com
Stainless steel
Alessi, Crusinallo, Italy

The only design created for Alessi by Marco Zanuso, the *Duna* cutlery range derived from an earlier flatware concept he had developed in 1960 for a competition held by Reed & Barton, an American cutlery company. The design's distinctive nipped-in section, described by Zanuso as a 'narrow waist', was intentionally reminiscent of the idealized 1950s homemaker's hourglass physique. Certainly, this dishwasher-safe design has a sensual and swelling form that invites interaction.

Kurve cutlery, 1963

Tapio Wirkkala (Finland, 1915–1985)

www.int.rosenthal.de
Stainless steel
Edelstahl
Acier inoxydable
Rosenthal, Selb, Germany

A gifted form giver, Tapio Wirkkala's work expressed his
deep understanding of the natural world, and was also
informed by his painstaking research into ergonomics. His
Kurve cutlery was designed to fit comfortably in the human
hand, and was the result of numerous studies and drawings
based on x-rays. Its ergonomically rational form is not only
pleasurable to hold, but is also extremely beautiful to look
at – a design that enchants the mind, hand and eye.

Carelia cutlery, 1963

Bertel Gardberg (Finland, 1916–2007)

www.hackman.fi
Stainless steel
Hackman/Iittala Group, Iittala, Finland

Bertel Gardberg specialized in the design of metalwares and jewellery, which won him international acclaim, numerous medals at the Milan Triennale exhibitions and also the Lunning Prize. His success owed to the fact that he could apply his finely honed craft skills to products intended for mass production, such as his famous *Carelia* flatware for Hackman. An acknowledged icon of Finnish design, the Carelia cutlery range has even featured on the country's postage stamps.

Zaha cutlery, 2007

Zaha Hadid (Iraq/UK, 1950–)

www.wmf.com
Stainless steel
WMF Württembergische Metallwarenfabrik,
Geislingen, Germany

Designed by the world-renowned architect, Zaha Hadid, this five-piece place setting echoes the vanguard dynamism of her extraordinary and sculptural buildings. The design's fluid and organic form belies its functional and ergonomic resolution. Distinctive and harmonious, the *Zaha* setting reflects WMF's belief that, 'Cutlery belongs within the category of tools that have the strongest and most intimate connection to their users, and whose design is shaped by manners, rituals and historical conventions.'

Balance cutlery, 1993

Matteo Thun (Germany, 1952–)

www.wmf.com
Stainless steel
WMF Württembergische Metallwarenfabrik, Geislingen, Germany

Matteo Thun's *Balance* cutlery is a modern yet timeless range that not only looks good but feels good too. As WMF explains: 'Soft contours, round shapes and balanced proportions produce the delicate and fascinating impression generated by this cutlery design. Sensual vibrancy and functionality are in perfect equilibrium with *Balance*.' This flatware range won a Design Plus award in 1993.

Skaugum cutlery, 1944

Uncredited (Norway)

www.skaugum.info
Teak, stainless steel
Skaugum/Geilo Jernvarefabrikk, Geilo, Norway

This classic range of cutlery is beautifully designed and exquisitely made. With a quality of construction one would expect from traditional Scandinavian craftsmanship, each handle is individually fitted and polished by hand. Available in either teak or rosewood, these handles are sourced from surplus woods set aside by the Norwegian furniture industry in order to reduce the environmental impact of their manufacture. Options with white or black acrylic handles are also available.

Citterio cutlery, 1998

Antonio Citterio (Italy, 1950–)

www.iittala.com
Stainless steel
Iittala, Iittala, Finland

Perfectly balanced and reassuringly weighty, this range of
cutlery feels wonderful in the hand. Part of Iittala's *Tools*
collection, *Citterio* flatware is not only functionally superlative but has a rare aesthetic refinement that distinguishes it
from other contemporary cutlery ranges. Furthermore, it is
so beautifully made that it will last a lifetime of daily use.

Mono Filio cutlery, 1990

Ralph Krämer (Germany, 1955–)

www.mono.de
Stainless steel
Mono/Seibel Designpartner, Mettmann, Germany

In the words of Ralph Krämer, 'Good design lies in achieving balance between tension and harmony' – a mission statement thoroughly realized in this flatware design. Inspired by the strict geometry of a trapezoid and the flowing movement of a wave, the *Mono Filio* range's comfort of use coexists with its sculptural eloquence.

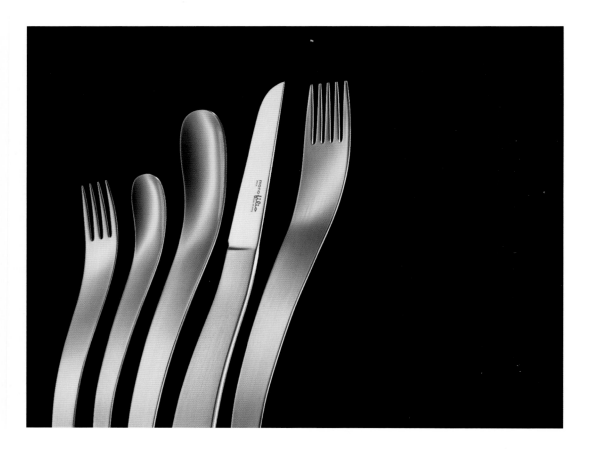

Mono-A cutlery, 1959

Peter Raacke (Germany, 1928–)

www.mono.de
Stainless steel or sterling silver
Mono/Seibel Designpartner, Mettmann, Germany

The *Mono-A* cutlery range was designed by Professor Peter Raacke in the late 1950s, and is generally considered a classic example of German design. With its clean and uncluttered lines, it certainly encapsulates its creator's functionalist approach to design. The *Mono-A* is the best-selling German flatware design of the postwar period, and continues to enjoy widespread popularity thanks to its aesthetic and functional purity.

Pott 42 cutlery, 2003

Ralph Krämer (Germany, 1955–)

www.pott–bestecke.de
Stainless steel
C Hugo Pott/Seibel Designpartner, Mettmann, Germany

In response to the recent trend for using larger and larger plates, Ralph Krämer made his *Pott 42* cutlery range a few centimetres longer than average flatware designs so as to achieve a better proportional balance on the table. Winning a Red Dot award in 2003, this visually striking design with its ergonomic fork and spoons, and its sabre-like knife, is characteristic of the bold functionalism and aesthetic purity of contemporary German design.

Pott 33 cutlery, 1975

Carl Pott (Germany, 1906–1985)

www.pott–bestecke.de
Stainless steel
C Hugo Pott/Seibel Designpartner, Mettmann, Germany

Pott began manufacturing high-quality knives in 1904. During the 1930s, the founder's son, Carl Pott – inspired by the teachings of the Bauhaus and the Deutscher Werkbund – began to design Modern-style cutlery remarkable for its functionalist forms. *Pott 33* flatware was one of his last designs, and encapsulates his pared-down style. When first introduced, his five-tined fork was seen as highly innovative, and with its slightly greater width over normal cutlery it certainly proved easier to use.

This beautiful cutlery range is a perfect example of the sensual elegance of 21st century organic design. As its title suggests, the *Tulipa's* form was inspired by the swelling shape of a budding tulip, giving the design a remarkable sense of sprouting growth. The organic forms of the different cutlery pieces are also ergonomically resolved, and sit comfortably in the hand as well as being reassuringly well balanced.

Tulipa cutlery, 2008

Jan Egeberg (Denmark, 1958–)
& Morten Thing (Denmark, 1954–)

www.gense.se
Stainless steel
Gense, Eskilstuna, Sweden

Folke Arström's *Focus de Luxe* is a classic Swedish design that reflects the widespread national belief that good design and quality of life are intertwined. Simple and beautiful, the *Focus* pattern expresses the casual sophistication of postwar Scandinavian design. It was especially successful in the United States, where it helped to associate formal dining with high-quality, Modern flatware in stainless steel, rather than with silverware in traditional patterns.

Focus de Luxe cutlery, 1955–1956

Folke Arström (Sweden, 1907–1997)

www.gense.se
Stainless steel
Gense, Eskilstuna, Sweden

Magnum cutlery, 1968

Don Wallance (USA, 1909–1990)

www.stelton.com
Stainless steel
Norstaal, Bergen, Norway/Stelton, Copenhagen, Denmark

Exquisitely balanced and perfectly formed to fit the hand, *Magnum* is Don Wallance's best-known cutlery range, and it is a tribute to his talent that it has remained in production for over forty years. With a no-nonsense robustness that is characteristically American, it also possesses an incredible ergonomic refinement. Almost forgotten today, Wallance was one of the greatest ever designers of flatware.

Maya cutlery, 1960

Tias Eckhoff (Norway, 1926–)

www.stelton.com
Stainless steel
Norstaal, Bergen, Norway/Stelton, Copenhagen, Denmark

An acknowledged icon of Norwegian design, the distinctive pattern of Tias Eckhoff's *Maya* flatware was inspired by ancient Mayan forms. This cutlery range is also comfortable and stable to use, thanks to its round-edged yet relatively flat handles. Since its launch in 1962, *Maya* has been a bestselling design, receiving the Norwegian Design Award in 1961, and the Classic Award for Design Excellence from the Norwegian Design Council in 1991.

Classic cutlery, 1994

David Mellor (UK, 1930–)

www.davidmellordesign.com
Stainless steel
David Mellor, Sheffield, UK

A timeless design with beautifully balanced proportions and careful detailing, Mellor's *Classic* flatware range looks as good in a traditional setting as it does in a modern environment. With a gentle and distinctive faceting around their handles, the nine pieces that make up the setting are comfortable to use and robust enough to give everyday service.

Provençal cutlery, 1973

David Mellor (UK, 1930–)

www.davidmellordesign.com
Stainless steel, acetal resin, brass rivets
David Mellor, Sheffield, UK

Throughout his illustrious career, David Mellor specialized in the design and manufacture of cutlery with superior performance characteristics. His influential *Provençal* design has an endearingly no-nonsense chunkiness, which was perfectly suited to the more casual lifestyle of the 1970s. It was also the first cutlery range to use handles made from moulded acetal – a rigid engineering plastic. Practical yet stylish, the eleven-piece range comes with a choice of black, blue or green handles.

Pride cutlery, 1953

David Mellor (UK, 1930–)

www.davidmellordesign.com
Silver-plated or stainless-steel blades, metal or acetal handles
David Mellor, Sheffield, UK

Widely acknowledged as a modern classic, *Pride* was David Mellor's first cutlery design and is also his most famous. Originally available only in silver plate, this flatware range is now also produced in stainless steel. Casual yet elegant, this eight-piece range epitomizes the understated sophistication of British design at its best.

Artik cutlery, 1997

Laura Partanen (Finland, 1972–)
& Arto Kankkunen (Finland, 1965–)

www.iittala.com
Stainless steel
Iittala, Iittala, Finland

According to its manufacturer, Iittala: '*Artik* is sophisticated design at its purest. The simplicity of the design's form is balanced by the sensual oval handles and the diagonal prongs of the fork. The solidity and weight convey a feeling of harmony and quality with every mouthful.' This extensive flatware range also includes a complimentary serving set, a thing of beauty in its own right.

Form 1382 tableware, 1931

Hermann Gretsch (Germany, 1895–1950)

www.arzberg-porzellan.de
Porcelain
Arzberg-Porzellan, Schimding, Germany

A landmark of German design, *1382* tableware was modern and affordable, and thereby embodied the Bauhaus' democratic ideals. In fact, its unadorned lines were guided foremost by functional considerations – one of Hermann Gretsch's main goals was to create a soup tureen that could be emptied using a ladle. The fact that the *1382* has been produced for over seventy-five years is testament to the enduring appeal of modern functionalism.

Sancerre dinnerware, 1983

Michel Roux (France, 1951–)

www.pillivuyt.fr
Porcelain
Pillivuyt, Mehun-sur-Yèvre, France

The porcelain manufacturer Pillivuyt has been producing fine tableware since 1818, and its *Sancerre* design is seen as *the* classic French, all-white dinner service among culinary *aficionados*. Timeless and durable, it has a stain-resistant glaze and eight different plate sizes, as well as numerous soup and pasta plates, serving and salad bowls, and accessories for coffee and tea. Robust enough for everyday use, the timeless, clean-looking *Sancerre* service is also microwave, oven and freezer safe.

Ku tableware, 2006

Toyo Ito (Japan, 1941–)

www.alessi.com
Porcelain
Alessi, Crusinallo, Italy

Toyo Ito, one of the world's most innovative and influential architects, designed this exquisite tableware service for Alessi – a company which, for decades, has enjoyed close working relationships with both world-class designers, and the most progressive architects. Like Ito's buildings, the *Ku* service, with its echoing and gently undulating forms, is an exquisite synthesis of form and material, and possesses a deeply poetic resonance.

Waen dinnerware, 2003

Kazuhiro Tominaga (Japan, active 1980s–2000s)

www1.ocn.ne.jp/~hakusan/hakusan-shop.htm
Glazed ceramic
Hakusan Porcelain Company, Nagasaki, Japan

Kazuhiro Tominaga studied craft design at Musashino Art University in Tokyo, graduating in 1982. In 1990, he joined the design office of the Hakusan Pottery Company, and has since won numerous awards for his simple and beautiful ceramic designs. His *Waen* range (which translates as 'Japanese Yen') is a series of inexpensive, high-fired, ceramic stacking dishes available in white, brown and black glazes. It won a Japanese Good Design award in 2003.

Origo tableware, 1999

Alfredo Häberli (Argentina/Switzerland, 1964–)

www.iittala.com
Porcelain
Iittala, Iittala, Finland

With its bold pattern of multicoloured stripes, Alfredo Häberli's *Origo* range of informal, everyday tableware was widely celebrated in the design press when first launched in 1999. Incorporating four sizes of bowls, two sizes of plates, an eggcup and a mug, the collection comes in various mix-and-match colour schemes giving a sense of freshness to any table. The range also works well with other tableware designs manufactured by Iittala, most notably the classic *Teema* collection designed by Kaj Franck in the late 1970s.

Teema tableware, 1977–1980

Kaj Frank (Finland, 1911–1989)

www.arabia.fi
Ceramic
Arabia/Iittala, Iittala, Finland

An evolution of Kaj Frank's earlier *Kilta* range from 1952, the *Teema* collection is a classic yet utilitarian tableware design based on simplification and essentialism. Using basic geometric forms – the circle, square and rectangle – Frank designed nineteen pieces that were to be used interchangeably with other items, rather than as a formal service. One of the great attractions of this highly versatile range is the way in which its variety of soft-toned colors can be endlessly combined and recombined.

Berså tableware, 1961

Stig Lindberg (Sweden, 1916–1982)

www.fabriksbutiken.com
Glazed ceramic
Gustavsberg, Gustavsberg, Sweden

Recently put back into production, Stig Lindberg's *Berså* tableware has a classic retro style with its repeating pattern of abstracted green leaves. Like much of Lindberg's work, it reminds one of a more innocent era, and has a child-like appeal. Moreover, unlike most patterned services, the *Berså* design also allows food to be attractively displayed, because its pattern is so stylishly simple. Although designed more than forty years ago, this service possesses a remarkable freshness that reflects a very Swedish celebration of nature.

The best-known manufacturer of Cornish Ware the TG Green pottery was founded by Thomas Goodwin Green in 1864, and produced plain earthenware designs for the home. In 1926, and in response to worsening economic times, the pottery decided to launch a more decorative range – its distinctively striped *Cornish Blue*. In 1966, a recent graduate from the Royal College of Art in London, Judith Onions, was enlisted to update this classic British design, and its continuing popularity is testament to its enduring popular appeal.

Cornish Blue kitchenware, 1966 (based on a design from 1926)

Judith Onions (UK, active 1960s)

www.tggreen.co.uk
Glazed ceramic
TG Green & Co, London, UK

Swedish Grace dinnerware, 1930

Louise Adelberg (Sweden, 1855–1971)

www.rorstrand.com
Porcelain
Rörstrand/Iittala Group, Höganäs, Sweden

This range of domestic tableware, with its simple repeating pressed pattern representing ears of wheat – a symbol of nourishment – was first exhibited at the landmark 1930 Stockholm Exhibition. Elegantly simple, this design came to epitomize 'Swedish Grace'– a term coined by the British architectural critic Morton Shand in the *Architectural Review*. This seminal Swedish design combines rustic charm with classical purity, and is available in a range of muted tones: cream, sage, pale blue and royal blue.

Suomi dinnerware, 1976

Timo Sarpaneva (Finland, 1926–2006)

www.int.rosenthal.de
Porcelain
Rosenthal, Selb, Germany

Suomi is a timeless yet stylishly modern dinner service that comprises an extensive number of pieces, ranging from a sushi plate to a chocolate mug. For its design, the tactile smoothness and soft organic forms of river pebbles inspired Timo Sarpaneva. In tribute to its high aesthetic and functional values the *Suomi* range was awarded the Gold Medal of Faenza – one of the highest accolades in the porcelain industry.

Moon dinnerware, 1997

Jasper Morrison (UK, 1959–)

www.int.rosenthal.de
Porcelain
Rosenthal, Selb, Germany

Throughout his career, Jasper Morrison has created objects that have an innate purity – both in terms of aesthetics and function. His *Moon* service exemplifies his essentialist approach to design, with its modern reworking of simple archetypal forms. As he explains, 'Design is not to demonstrate the unusual. Only one thing counts: it must function'. In tribute to this product's inherent 'rightness', it won a Red Dot award in 2002 and an iF award in 2003.

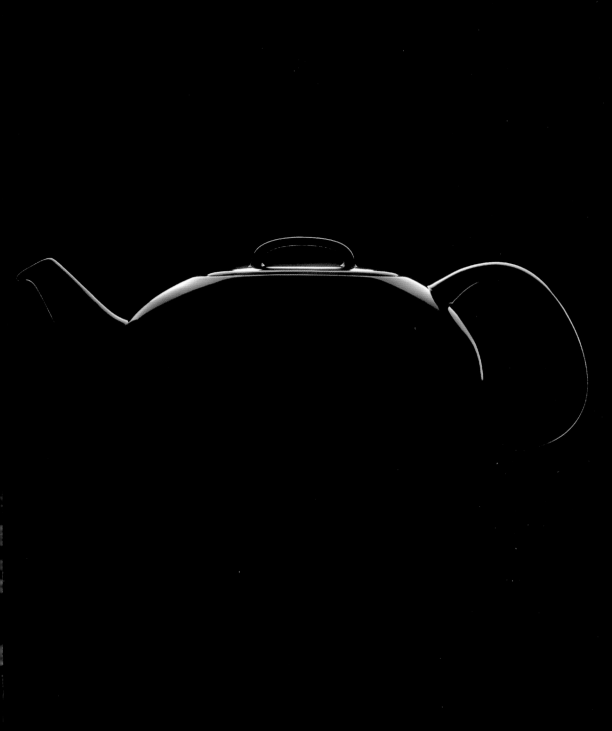

Crested Porcelain tableware, 1988

Sori Yanagi (Japan, 1915–)

www.soriyanagi.com
Glazed porcelain
Sori Yanagi, Valby, Denmark

Sori Yanagi's tableware combines practical function with an understated elegance, which expresses the very Japanese love of harmonious balance and exquisite detailing. His *Crested Porcelain* range has a strikingly formal simplicity that is subtly embellished with abstracted decorative motifs that create associations with the centuries-old *marumon* and *musubimon* patterns used as family crests in Japan. Dishwasher and microwave-safe, this stacking tableware range brings a much-needed touch of oriental refinement into our daily environment.

Semiglazed tableware, 1982

Sori Yanagi (Japan, 1915–)

www.soriyanagi.com
Ceramic
Sori Yanagi, Valby, Denmark

The matt surface of Sori Yanagi's *Semiglazed* tableware range gives a soft and appealing appearance that invites physical interaction. Available in black or white, a special production method is used so that the semi-glazed ceramic material is much lighter than traditional earthenware, while at the same time remaining more robust than porcelain. The soft contours of the individual pieces also enhance their sensual fluidity, and ensure that they fit comfortably in the hands.

Spir gravy boats, 2002

Johan Verde (Norway, 1964–)

www.figgjo.no
Porcelain
↕ 12, 14 cm
Figgjo, Figgjo, Norway

Part of Johan Verde's award-winning *Spir* range, these sculptural gravy boats come in two sizes. Although their organic form is reminiscent of the biomorphic shapes that were so popular in the 1950s, the timeless elegance of these designs ensure that they compliment Figgjo's other tableware products. Like other designs by Johan Verde, their contours are based on the idea of an encircling 'fold', such as those found in the spirals of seashells.

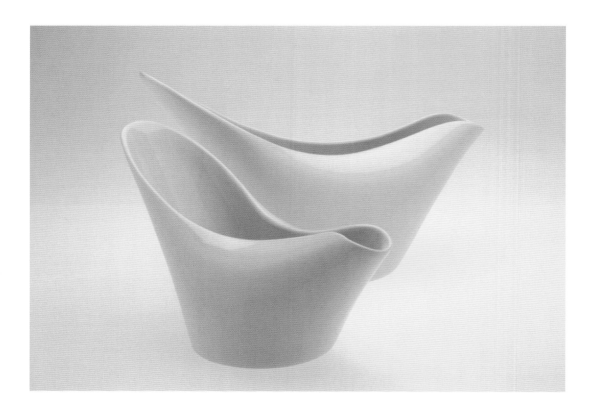

Form 2000 dinnerware, 1954

Heinrich Löffelhardt (Germany, 1901–1979)

www.arzberg–porzellan.de
Porcelain
Arzberg-Porzellan, Schirnding, Germany

Although inspired by Hermann Gretsch's earlier *1382* dinner service for Arzberg, Heinrich Löffelhardt's *Form 2000* range is less utilitarian and more elegant than its famous predecessor. Its soft, ergonomic form also reflects the increasing influence of organic shapes during the 1950s. In fact, Löffelhardt regarded each piece of the service as a sculpture in its own right. In recognition of its 'good design' credentials, the *Form 2000* service received a gold medal at the 1954 Milan Triennale.

Ursula jug, 1992
Ursula Munch-Petersen (Denmark, 1937–)

www.royalcopenhagen.com
Porcelain or faience
0.3l, 0.5l, 1 l
Royal Copenhagen, Copenhagen, Denmark

Available in three sizes, this distinctive jug compliments
the rest of the *Ursula* dinner service, which was designed
by Ursula Munch-Petersen in 1992. According to Royal
Copenhagen, she 'thought out each piece as an independent
entity, and the function of the items is precisely reflected
in their vigorous, rounded shapes. She feels that everyday
items should reflect people. A handle must almost ask to be
gripped'. Munch-Petersen also believes that design should
be imbued with a handicraft sensibility even when it relates
to mass-production.

Blue Line cream jug & cover, 1965

Grethe Meyer (Denmark, 1918–)

www.royalcopenhagen.com
Porcelain
0.14 l
Royal Copenhagen, Copenhagen, Denmark

Between 1955 and 1960, Grethe Meyer painstakingly
examined the standard dimensions used in housing and
consumer products. This early research, as well as her
desire to make 'things people can afford', informed her
later design of utilitarian housewares, including her *Blue
Line* service designed for Royal Copenhagen. This range of
ceramics (which includes the cream jug, shown below) with
its endearing simplicity borne out of practical functionality,
demonstrated her mastery of form as well as her understanding of industrial production.

Ole pitcher/citrus press, 1997

Ole Jensen (Denmark, 1958–)

www.royalcopenhagen.com
Porcelain or faience
Royal Copenhagen, Copenhagen, Denmark

One of the leading lights of contemporary Danish design, Ole Jensen has won numerous accolades for his everyday products that playfully challenge the *status quo*. His *Ole* jug-cum-juicer is a sculptural design that serves its intended function well: the jug's narrow spout traps any pips or pulp, while its integrated hand-hold and rounded base ensure that it is comfortable to use. The white version is made of porcelain, and the coloured options are made of faience – a glazed earthenware.

EgO tableware, 1998

Stefan Lindfors (Finland, 1962–)

www.iittala.com
Porcelain
Iittala, Iittala, Finland

Stefan Lindfors's *EgO* range initially comprised an espresso cup, a coffee cup and a breakfast cup, as well as a matching bowl and pitcher. The relatively large-scale saucers that go with these cups are perfect for the serving of an accompanying chocolate, biscuit or pastry. They are also very stable and steady in the hand. Perfect for today's international coffee culture, the *EgO* is a design perfectly in tune with contemporary living. In 2000, additional elements, including large plates and various containers for spices, were also added to the range.

Contrast cup, 2007

Hans Christian Gjedde (Denmark, 1970–)

www.royalcopenhagen.com
Porcelain, silicone
Royal Copenhagen, Copenhagen, Denmark

Although harking back to the ancient oriental tradition of
tea drinking, Hans Christian Gjedde's *Contrast* cups have
a very 21st century twist with their use of pastel-coloured
silicone covers that help to protect fingers from burning. As
Niels Bastrup, the creative director at Royal Copenhagen,
explains: 'Porcelain is perfect for combining with other
materials…Royal Copenhagen is world famous for exploring
and expanding the potential of porcelain, and with *Contrast*
we've dared to take a step in a new direction, with porcelain making up the core of the product, while the colourful
silicone cover is the star guest'.

Figgjo Verde mug, 1995

Johan Verde (Norway, 1964–)

www.figgjo.no
Porcelain
Figgjo, Figgjo, Norway

This diminutive mug is part of the *Figgjo Verde* service, which won the Norwegian Award for Design Excellence in 1996. This functional yet elegant mug is, in fact, one of the manufacturer's most popular products, and as such is found in cafés across Norway. Although possessing a strong Scandinavian Modern aesthetic, the design's Essentialist form also references Oriental Minimalism, and perfectly balances form with utility in the process.

Java mug, 2008

Åsa Lindberg Svensson (Sweden, 1972–)

www.sagaform.com
Stoneware
Sagaform, Borås, Sweden

This stoneware mug comes in a white, black, linen or blue glaze, and can be stacked for efficient storage. Like other designs produced by Sagaform, it has a practical utility and aesthetic purity that epitomizes modern Scandinavian design, deservedly famed for its human-centric approach to everyday housewares. Indeed, there is a long-held Nordic belief that well-designed and user-friendly objects can be life enhancing tools for social change – yes, even a humble mug!

Noguchi teacup & saucer, 1952

Isamu Noguchi (USA, 1904–1988)

www.design-museum.de
Porcelain
Vitra Design Museum, Weil am Rhein, Germany

Although designed by Isamu Noguchi in 1952, this beautiful, almost zoomorphic teacup was only very recently put into production. Noguchi learnt the skilful handling of ceramics from one of Japan's most acclaimed potters, Rosanjin Kitaoji. It was when Noguchi was living in Kitaoji's compound of traditional buildings in Kita Kamakura that he modelled this curious, horn-handled cup from clay. Its form was based on an old terracotta cup owned by Noguchi himself.

Bistro mug, 2006

Bodum Design Group

www.bodum.com
Glass or porcelain
Bodum, Triengen, Switzerland

The *Bistro* series comprises an espresso cup, a café latte cup, a regular mug (as shown below), an extra-large mug and three sizes of glasses. The series is available in either double-walled, transparent glass or white porcelain. Also known as the *Corona* range in some countries, the timeless and casual elegance of these functional designs won them a prestigious iF product design award in 2007.

Bora Bora teapot, 2005

Bodum Design Group

www.bodum.com
Borosilicate glass, stainless steel
0.5 l
Bodum, Triengen, Switzerland

Designed to keep your tea hotter for longer, the award-winning *Bora Bora* teapot has a double-walled glass construction to promote the retention of heat. This innovative design also improves the taste of the tea by incorporating Bodum's patented tea press system, which uses a plunger to stop the brewing process once the tea has been steeped to the required strength. The good news for tea drinkers is that this eliminates the tannic bitterness of 'stewed' tea.

Helena tea set, 2007

Helena Rohner (Spain, 1968–)

www.georgjensen.com
Polished stainless steel, porcelain
Georg Jensen, Copenhagen, Denmark

One of Spain's most acclaimed jewellery designers, Helena Rohner's work is characterized by simple elemental forms and interesting combinations of materials. The *Helena* tea set is no exception, with its contemporary twist on the traditional tea service. As the designer explains, 'The round shape of the teapot reminded me of a steamship with its slightly pointed and sloping design. The combination of porcelain and stainless steel gives a soft yet modern appearance.'

Brown Betty teapot, c. 1680s–1840s

Anonymous (UK)

www.cauldonceramics.co.uk
Glazed ceramic
2 cup, 4 cup, 6 cup, 8 cup
Cauldron Ceramics, Stoke-on-Trent, UK

This classic, chestnut-brown, glazed English teapot – some-times known as the *Brown Betty* – is a wonderful example of anonymous design. Between the late 17th century and the 1840s, this traditional round-bellied teapot evolved to such a high degree that it achieved an exceptional fitness for purpose – it pours well, brews tea to perfection and does not stain. Manufactured by a number of British companies, the *Brown Betty* is a generic and un-improvable design, and if you like a strong 'brew' this is definitely the pot for you.

Harp teapot, 2004

Ichiro Iwasaki (Japan, 1965–)

www.ricordi–sfera.com
Porcelain, natural or black stained maple plywood
Sfera, Kyoto Japan

Winning a prestigious Red Dot award in 2007, the *Harp* teapot is a synthesis of English and Japanese tea-drinking traditions. In fact, English tea is now very much a part of everyday life in Japan, and this hybrid design – an English teapot with a Japanese aesthetic – reflects the global cross-pollination of cultures in the 21st century. Suitable for making both English and Japanese tea, this design possesses a sense of both modernity and timelessness.

Tea service, 1931

Wilhelm Wagenfeld (Germany, 1900–1990)

www.jenaer–glas.com
Heat-resistant borosilicate glass
Schott Jenaer Glas/Zwiesel Kristallglas, Zwiesel, Germany

A classic Bauhaus design, Wilhelm Wagenfeld's elegant transparent tea set is made from borosilicate glass, which was initially developed for laboratory use, and is heat-resistant up to 450 °C (779 °F). Wagenfeld chose a hand-blown moulding technique that enabled the glass to be stretched particularly thinly, giving the tea service a remarkable visual and physical lightness. With its stripped-down, essentialist aesthetic, this design has a distinctive Modernity.

Ciacapo teapot, 2000

Kazuhiko Tomita (Japan, 1965–)

www.covo.com
Cast iron
0.6, 1 l
Covo, Formello, Italy

A contemporary interpretation of the traditional Japanese *tetsubin*, Kazuhiko Tomita's *Ciacapo* teapot combines high-quality craftsmanship with a simple and modern form. As a Japanese designer working in Milan, he is able to synthesize cultural influences from both East and West to create poetic objects that are both aesthetically satisfying and functional. Unlike many traditional Japanese teapots, this design has a spout that always points upwards, which means it is easier to pour.

Sicamba trivet, 2000

Kazuhiko Tomita (Japan, 1965–)

www.covo.com
Cast iron
↔ 32 cm
Covo, Formello, Italy

Effortlessly fusing the design sensibilities of East and West, Kazuhiko Tomita's *Sicamba* trivet for Covo takes its scrolling, leaf-like form from a traditional Japanese decorative arabesque pattern, known as *karakusa*. Available in four muted colours, this weighty, cast-iron trivet will last forever, and when several are grouped together on a table they produce a pleasing panel-like effect.

Warm tea set, 1998

Brian Keaney (Ireland, 1974–) & Tony Alfström (Finland, 1972–)

www.tonfisk-design.fi
Porcelain, laminated oak, laminated walnut or cork
Tonfisk Design, Turku, Finland

Brian Keaney's motivation for designing this product was a straightforward one: he drinks a great deal of tea. Keaney recalls, however, that at the time he, 'preferred mugs [without handles] to cups with handles. Unfortunately though my father complained that they burned his fingers. Then a fellow student was participating on a materials course where at one stage the wood laminating technique was examined, and this introduced me to its possibilities and so a [handle-less] mug which doesn't burn your fingers was developed'. Since its introduction in 1998, various additional pieces have been added to the range, and a black version has also been produced.

Teamaster tea service, 2004

Jasper Morrison (UK, 1959–)

www.idee.co.jp
Porcelain
Nikko/Idee, Tokyo, Japan

Designed specifically for the Japanese market, the *Teamaster* is a modern reworking of a traditional Japanese tea set. There is something very special about the way Jasper Morrison manages to create simple objects whose stripped-down essentialist forms lend an extra aesthetic dimension. With Naoto Fukasawa, Morrison has coined the term 'supernormal' to describe ordinary objects that transcend the everyday, and the *Teamaster* is an exemplary realization of this concept.

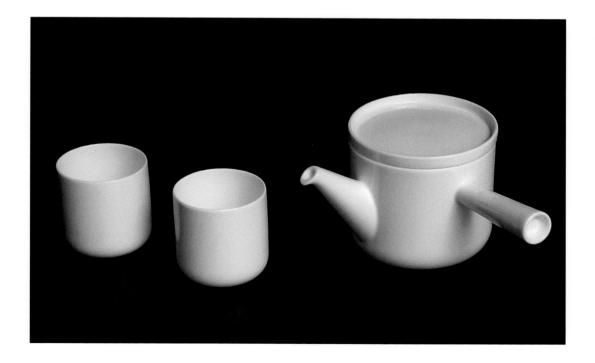

TAC tea set, 1969

Walter Gropius (Germany, 1883–1969)

www.int.rosenthal.de
Porcelain
Rosenthal, Selb, Germany

The founding director of the famous Bauhaus design school, Walter Gropius went onto to found The Architects+ Collaborative (TAC) architectural practice in Cambridge, Massachusetts in 1945. Apart from various landmark buildings, Gropius also designed the TAC tea service, which is part of Rosenthal's renowned *Studio-Line* range, prized for its innovative aesthetics and functional originality. These values are embedded in the design's quasi-streamlined form, which was inspired by symmetrical reflections. The separate pieces are available in either black or white porcelain, and can be combined to create an interesting visual contrast.

Spir tea & coffee set, 2002

Johan Verde (Norway, 1964–)

www.figgjo.no
Porcelain
Figgjo, Figgjo, Norway

Receiving the Award for Design Excellence from the Norwegian Design Council in 2003, the *Spir* tea and coffee set comprises seven mix-and-match pieces: three coffee/tea pots, three cream jugs and a sugar bowl. Intended to compliment Figgjo's existing white tableware, this range was based on Johan Verde's concept of 'complex simplicity'. It was developed using CAD software which, according to Verde, 'makes possible nearly any thinkable form', allowing 'form to be transformed into matter'.

Although *La Cafetière* is often viewed as *the* classic French coffee maker, the plunger/filter system it employs was actually developed in Italy in the late 1920s. It was, however, a French company, Société des Anciens Etablissements Martin, that patented this classic coffee press in the 1950s, distributing it under the name *Chambord*. From the early 1960s onwards a British business, Household Articles Limited, marketed the design with the trade name *La Cafetière*. Thanks to its huge sales success, *'cafetière'* has now become the generic British term for plunge/filter coffee makers.

La Cafetière coffee press, 1950s

Société des Anciens Établissements Martin (France)

www.lacafetiere.com
Chrome-plated or gold-plated stainless steel, heat-resistant glass, plastic
3 cup, 4 cup, 8 cup, 12 cup
La Cafetière, Greenfield, Flintshire, uk

Moka Express espresso maker, 1933

Alfonso Bialetti (Italy, 1888–1970)

www.bialetti.it
Aluminium, Bakelite
3 cup, 6 cup, 9 cup, 12 cup
Bialetti Industrie, Coccaglio, Italy

The classic Italian espresso maker, the *Moka Express* is a stovetop coffee pot which introduced steam pressure into coffee making. The design has three main components: a lower, water-holding section which acts as a boiler; a funnel-shaped metal filter in the central section which contains the ground coffee; and an upper, jug-like section where the freshly brewed liquid collects, and from which it can be poured. Inexpensive, the faceted Art Deco *Moka Express* is an iconic Italian design that brings a *Dolce Vita* ambience to any kitchen. It makes great coffee too.

Coffee filter & coffee pot, 1937

Melitta Bentz (Germany, 1873–1950)

www.melitta.com
Porcelain
6 cup
Melitta Beratungs-und Verwaltungsgesellschaft, Minden, Germany

A classic German design, this utilitarian coffee funnel and pot were designed by Melitta Bentz, a Dresden housewife who experimented with her children's blotting paper to produce a properly filtered drink. She patented her famous filtering system in 1908, and in 1937 the now ubiquitous Melitta coffee-filtering bags were developed. They could be used in conjunction with the company's white porcelain funnel and pot whose attractive yet unadorned forms reflected the influence of Bauhaus Modernism.

Probably Ole Palsby's best-known design, and certainly his most commercially successful product, the *Classic No.1* thermal jug not only works exceptionally well but also possesses a timeless grace. In fact, its form is an accomplished modern reinterpretation of traditional Channel Island milk 'cans' or 'creamers'. This updating of a vernacular design typology in order to create an 'ideal product' has long been a strong characteristic of Danish design, and in Palsby's career a guiding principle.

Classic No.1 thermal jug, 1985

Ole Palsby (Denmark, 1935–)

www.alfi.de
ABS, mirrored glass
0.94 l
Alfi, Wertheim, Germany

Available in four colours – cobalt blue, white, anthracite grey and lava-red – the *Basic* thermal vacuum flask has a 0.9 litre capacity and can be used for both hot and cold drinks. Visually seductive and technologically persuasive, with its transparent scratchproof acrylic casing protecting its silvered liner, the *Basic* carafe inspired a major trend towards transparency in product design. When launched, the design was named Product of the Year by the Fachverband Kunststoff Konsumwaren, and also won the Sonderschau Form Prize at Tendence Frankfurt.

Basic vacuum flask, 1990

Julian Brown (UK, 1955–)
& Ross Lovegrove (UK, 1958–)

www.alfi.de
PMMA, mirrored glass
0.9 l
Alfi, Wertheim, Germany

Thermal Carafe, 1976

Erik Magnussen (Denmark, 1940–)

www.stelton.com
ABS, glass
0.5, 1 l
Stelton, Copenhagen, Denmark

Originally intended to compliment Arne Jacobsen's earlier *Cylinda Line* range for Stelton, Erik Magnussen's elegant and practical insulated jug is produced with either a stainless steel or brightly coloured ABS plastic body. Exemplifying some of the key characteristics of Magnussen's design, and available in various colours, the *Thermal Carafe* has a functional and aesthetically pleasing durability that has ensured its appeal for over thirty years. Like other classic icons of Danish design, this highly successful thermos jug has a sophisticated simplicity that makes it both pleasurable to use and easy to manufacture.

Pingo vacuum jug, 2005

John Sebastian (Denmark, 1975–)

www.stelton.com
Stainless steel, plastic
0.25 l, 1 l
Stelton, Copenhagen, Denmark

Following the huge success of Erik Magnussen's 1970s thermal jug, Stelton recently introduced an evolution of this theme: John Sebastian's *Pingo* vacuum jug, with its distinctive, penguin-like form. Available in two sizes – one litre and 0.25 litre – the design is a sleek reworking of a traditional picnic vacuum jug. Moreover, its 'beak' incorporates new technology that ensures it is both completely childproof, and will not leak when lying flat. This innovative product has won a prestigious iF product design award, and a Design Plus award.

Ole thermal jug, 1997

Ole Jensen (Denmark, 1958–)

www.royalcopenhagen.com
Porcelain or faience
1 l
Royal Copenhagen, Copenhagen, Denmark

This sculptural thermal jug has an engagingly organic form that invites caressing. Designed to compliment Ole Jensen's innovative *Ole* dinnerware range, this dishwasher-safe jug has an elongated spout that makes it easy to pour. With its distinctive rounded base, it also has a low centre of gravity that gives stability to the design. This pleasing product is a clever and stylish reworking of the traditional thermal jug.

Quack insulated jug, 2003

Maria Berntsen (Denmark, 1961–)

www.georgjensen.com
ABS, polyurethane, aluminium
0.9 l
Georg Jensen, Copenhagen, Denmark

Named after its engaging, duck-like form, the
Quack insulated jug won a Red Dot Best of the
Best award in 2003. Available in brown, green
or beige, it keeps liquids warm for up to four
hours, and can also be used for cold drinks. As
Maria Berntsen explains, 'A shape should awake
feelings and tell a story. A thing should never
just be a thing. A body or sculpture…[has]
shapes I never tire of looking at. I hope my
designs awake the same emotions'.

AJ Cylinda Line tea & coffee service, 1967

Arne Jacobsen (Denmark, 1902–1971)

www.stelton.com
Stainless steel, thermoset plastic
Stelton, Copenhagen, Denmark

Stelton produced the *AJ Cylinda Line* range, including this tea and coffee set, from some 'terse, logical and functional' drawings of cylindrical forms sketched by Arne Jacobsen in 1964. At the time, the technology required to translate these drawings into three-dimensional products did not exist. In order to manufacture these classic hollow-ware designs (which were launched in 1967), Stelton therefore had to develop a variety of new machines and welding techniques.

Opus carafe, 2007

Ole Palsby (Denmark, 1935–)

www.rosendahl.dk
Glass
Rosendahl, Hørsholm, Denmark

Believing throughout his career that 'design should be for the hand and the eye', Ole Palsby has created useful, beautiful and simple objects for the home. This award-winning carafe is part of his *Opus* range, which grew from the principle that function should determine the choice of material – in this case, clear glass. Thanks to its size and shape, the carafe can be cooled in a fridge door, while its airtight stopper ensures freshness.

Canasta fruit bowl, 2008

Emiliano Godoy (Mexico, 1974–)

www.nouvelstudio.com
Glass
∅ 21.7 cm
Nouvel Studio, Naucalpan, Mexico

Available in aqua green, ruby red, smoky topaz, olive green, amber and clear glass, the *Canasta* fruit bowl is an attractive design that can be carried to a tabletop almost like a basket – indeed, its name means 'basket' in Spanish. Godoy created this design using old manufacturers' moulds, which he then modified. The concept of recycling and then adapting moulds is a novel one, and it allows Godoy to create new designs in a highly sustainable way.

Free Spirit bowl, 2004

Robin Platt (UK, 1962–)

www.rosenthal.de
Porcelain
Rosenthal AG, Selb, Germany

The *Free Spirit* dish is part of a range of serving wares designed by Robin Platt for Rosenthal's well-known *Studio-Line* collection. These dishes also compliment Platt's extensive porcelain dinner service bearing the same name, which shares the same abstracted biomorphic free forms. As its name suggests, the *Free Sprit* range is intended to be functionally flexible and the antithesis of traditional and overly formal dinner services.

Butterfly bowl, c. 1951

Richard K Thomas (USA, active 1950s)

www.nambe.com
Nambé alloy
Nambé, Santa Fe (NM), USA

During the Manhattan Project in the 1940s, a new proprietary metal alloy (given the name Nambé) was developed at the Los Alamos National Laboratory, which was capable of retaining heat and cold for long periods of time. In 1951, Nambé Ware Mills was established to produce home wares from this new silver-like, non-tarnishing, eight-metal alloy. Richard K Thomas, a sculptor, created some of the company's early designs, including the *Butterfly* bowl, which epitomizes the bold sculptural forms that marked American design during the 1950s.

Model No. 4505 Collection serving bowl with handles, 1996

Lovisa Wattman (Sweden, 1967–)

www.hoganaskeramik.se
Glazed earthenware
2 l
Höganäs Keramik/Iittala Group, Höganäs, Sweden

Available in nine colours, this attractive serving bowl
expresses the long-held Nordic belief that beautiful
everyday objects can enrich life. With its soft organic form,
this design invites physical interaction, while its handles
enable it to be carried easily to the table. Specializing in the
design of kitchenware and tableware, Lovisa Wattman is a
true *formgivare* – the Swedish term for 'designer' that can
be translated still more directly as 'form giver'.

Concept salad bowl, 2000s

Jenaer Glas Design Team

www.jenaer-glas.com
Heat-resistant glass
2 l, 4 l
Jenaer Glas/Zwiesel Kristallglas, Zwiesel, Germany

In 1884, the chemist Otto Schott, together with Carl Zeiss and his son Roderich, established a glass research laboratory in Jena that developed the world's first ovenproof household glass. Their glassworks subsequently worked with Bauhaus designers to create functional objects for the kitchen. It was in this tradition that the *Concept Collection* by Jenaer Glas (including the salad bowl shown here) was devised, conceived as adding a few timeless, everyday 'basics' to the kitchen environment.

Saladia bowls, 2001

Kazuhiko Tomita (Japan, 1965–)

www.covo.com
Matt-glazed ceramic
Covo, Formello, Italy

These elegant bowls combine a matt rust glaze with a shiny black or cream glaze in order to create an interesting textural quality, while their soft curves also make them pleasant to hold. Essentially a modern reworking of a traditional Japanese noodle bowl, the *Saladia* is an understated design that goes beyond simple practicality with its purity of form and tactility. Like other designs by Kazuhiko Tomita, the *Saladia* is a 'quiet object' of great refinement, representative of the aesthetic and functional sensitivity of Japanese home wares.

Krenit bowl & Krenit salad bowl, 1953

Herbert Krenchel (Denmark, 1922–)

www.normann-copenhagen.com
Enamelled iron
⌀ 25, 38 cm
Normann Copenhagen, Copenhagen, Denmark

As the design-engineer, Herbert Krenchel, explains, "In 1953, the idea was to make a beautiful bowl, preferably so functional and delicate that it was equally suited for use in the kitchen, on the dining table and as a decoration in the sitting room. As a material researcher I really concentrated on getting the different materials to match and look good together, as well as making them equally compatible to use together." Having recently been reissued, these much-loved icons of Danish design are accessible once more.

Small bowl with spoon, 2008

Peter Moritz (Sweden, 1964–) & Eva Moritz (Sweden, 1966–)

www.sagaform.com
Bamboo
⌀ 13 cm
Sagaform, Borås, Sweden

One can almost imagine this bowl being used by Goldilocks when she sampled the bears' porridge. It certainly has a reassuringly rustic quality, with its use of two-tone bamboo. Yet, at the same time, it has a contemporary sculptural elegance and a functional logic, especially in the way the spoon's indentation 'locks' it to the rim of the bowl for one-handed carrying.

Large serving bowl, 2008

Peter Moritz (Sweden, 1964–) & Eva Moritz (Sweden, 1966–)

www.sagaform.com
Bamboo
ø 26 cm
Sagaform, Borås, Sweden

A good and environmentally friendly alternative to the
ubiquitous teak salad bowl, this large-size serving bowl is
made of sustainably grown bamboo. Its lightweight port-
ability and two-tone colour scheme attractively differentiate
it from your average salad bowl design – a simple, yet subtly
different eco-design.

Chip & Dip bowl, 2006

Tom Sullivan (USA, 1957–) & Joanne Chen (USA, 1952–)

www.totallybamboo.com
Bamboo
Ø 34 cm
Totally Bamboo, San Marcos (CA), USA

Although bamboo has been used to make household products in the Far East for millennia, it is only in the last decade or so that it has become a more viable manufacturing material in the West. This *Chip & Dip* bowl is made from laminated strips of bamboo and, although light in weight, it is surprisingly strong. In fact, bamboo is denser than most hardwoods, but has a re-harvesting cycle of less than five years, whereas most hardwoods take between thirty and sixty years to reach maturity.

Super Big bowl, 2006

Tom Sullivan (USA, 1957–) & Joanne Chen (USA, 1952–)

www.totallybamboo.com
Bamboo
∅ 34 cm
Totally Bamboo, San Marcos (CA), USA

One hundred per cent renewable, bamboo is the most sustainable and eco-friendly wood-type material available to designers, manufacturers, and consumers. This large and elegant serving bowl demonstrates that stylish houseware designs can be made from this ecologically renewable alternative to hardwoods. Not only is it better for the environment, but the abundance and sustainability of bamboo also make it less expensive to produce.

Round bowls, 2001

Tom Sullivan (USA, 1957–) & Joanne Chen (USA, 1952–)

www.totallybamboo.com
Bamboo
Totally Bamboo, San Marcos (CA), USA

A few years ago, Tom Sullivan and Joanne Chen set up a design and manufacturing studio in north Hollywood, and began producing customized director's chairs. Trying to make their chairs ever lighter, they began experimenting with bamboo and were impressed with its strength-to-weight ratio as well as its ecological credentials. Shortly afterwards, they established their own company, Totally Bamboo, producing housewares – such as the bowls shown here – made to their own designs from this remarkable, renewable material.

101001 large cork bowl & 101101 low cork bowl, 2009

Rachel Speth (USA, 1962–)

www.bambuhome.com
Untreated cork
↕ 10 cm ⌀ 30.5 cm
↕ 6 cm ⌀ 30.5 cm
Bambu, Mineola (NY), USA

A popular material in the late 1970s, cork is now experiencing something of a renaissance thanks to its eco-friendly credentials. An impermeable, buoyant and fire-resistant material stripped from the trunks of cork oak trees, it has a multitude of uses from champagne stoppers to floor tiles. These two bowls – designed by the co-founder of Bambu, Rachel Speth – are made from cork that is sustainably harvested without harming the tree. Interestingly this durable, lightweight and slip-resistant material is also naturally hypo-allergenic, anti-microbial, and anti-fungal.

Salad servers, 2008

Peter Moritz (Sweden, 1964–) & Eva Moritz (Sweden, 1966–)

www.sagaform.com
Bamboo
↕ 33 cm
Sagaform, Borås, Sweden

Both Peter and Eva Moritz studied at the Konstfack – the University College of Arts, Crafts and Design in Stockholm – before establishing their own design studio in Lund in 1998. Since then, they have specialized in the design of house-hold objects and furniture for mass production, while also pursuing more craft-related projects. Their distinctive designs have a strong sculptural quality, as is demon-strated by these salad servers for Sagaform, which are made of sustainably grown bamboo.

Butter knife, 2008

Peter Moritz (Sweden, 1964–) & Eva Moritz (Sweden, 1966–)

www.sagaform.com
Bamboo
↔ 17.5 cm
Sagaform, Borås, Sweden

Made of sustainably harvested bamboo, this butter knife is sold as a set of two. Its rounded, organic form makes it perfect for spreading butter, margarine, jam or indeed anything you might want on your daily bread. Like other designs by Peter and Eva Moritz, this simple tool for living reveals a very human-centric and sensual approach to design.

Caravel salad servers, 1957

Henning Koppel (Denmark, 1918–1981)

www.georgjensen.com
Stainless steel, polycarbonate
Georg Jensen, Copenhagen, Denmark

These elegant salad servers were originally manufactured in silver to compliment Henning Koppel's *Caravel* flatware collection, which won the prestigious Der goldene Löffel award in 1963. Today, however, they are made from stainless steel and plastic, and a matching salad bowl designed by Koppel in the 1970s has also been produced. With their fluid and unadorned lines, the *Caravel* salad servers have a timeless appeal and typify the understated sophistication of Koppel's sculptural design language.

Mono-C2 salad servers, 2004

Ute Schniedermann (Germany, 1959–)

www.mono.de
Stainless steel
Mono/Seibel Designpartner, Mettmann, Germany

These classic salad servers will grace any table with their elegantly modern aesthetic. They epitomize the manufacturing quality, the painstaking attention to engineering detail, and the rigorous focus on function which, over the decades, we have come to expect from German housewares. Above all, these salad servers are a sublime example of contemporary German design.

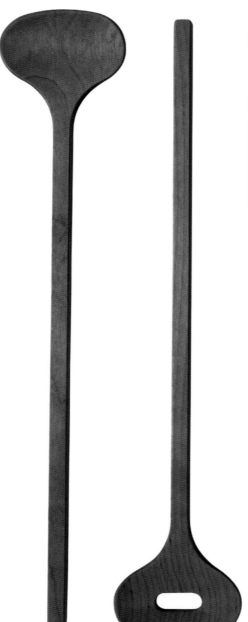

Tools salad servers, 1998
Carina Seth-Andersson (Denmark, 1965–)

www.iittala.com
Heat-treated birch
↕ 36 cm
Iittala, Iittala, Finland

Only recently put back into production, Carina Seth-Andersson's *Tools* salad servers are an exquisite example of Scandinavian design at its very best. Harmoniously balanced, and beautifully crafted from heat-treated birch, they are extremely comfortable to handle and go well with almost any modern-style salad bowl. Like other designs from Iittala's *Tools* range, these salad servers have an appealing organic essentialism.

Good Grips serving tongs, 1997

Smart Design (USA, est. 1978)

www.oxo.com
Stainless steel, Santoprene
↔ 34.5 cm
OXO International, New York (NY), USA

These sturdy tongs are made of high-quality
stainless steel and, like other products created
by Smart Design for OXO, their superior ergonomic refinement means that users of almost
any physical ability can use them comfortably
and safely. The Santoprene elastomeric grips
also provide stability when serving anything
from salad to chicken.

Selandia dish, 1952

Per Lütken (Denmark, 1916–1998)

www.holmegaard.com
Glass
↔ 31 cm
Holmegaard Glasværk, Holmegaard, Denmark

Inspired by traditional glassmaking techniques, the circular motion of a spinning glassblower's pipe makes the appealing organic form of the *Selandia* dish, which is available in clear, blue and smoked glass variants. Driven by, 'A feeling for glass. A feeling for glassmaking. A feeling for what people need', Per Lütken worked as a designer for Holmegaard for more than fifty years and created over 3,000 glassware designs, with the *Selandia* being, perhaps, the most iconic of his oeuvre.

Provence bowl, c. 1956

Per Lütken (Denmark, 1916–1998)

www.holmegaard.com
Glass
⌀ 13, 19, 25, 31 cm
Holmegaard Glasværk, Holmegaard, Denmark

An acclaimed classic of Danish Modernism, the *Provence* bowl, with its beautifully curved form, reflects Per Lütken's sheer mastery of form and material. Capturing the spiritual essence of molten glass with its soft, undulating shape, the *Provence* bowl also came to epitomize the gentle organic forms that were to dominate Scandinavian design during the postwar period. Holmegaard produces four different versions of the design: clear, blue, green and smoked glass.

With its abstracted, bird-like form, Henning Koppel's *992* jug is an iconic Mid-Century design. Like other designs by this master form giver, its organic shape accentuates the gleaming qualities of the silver, while its flowing lines make the metal appear almost molten. Imbued with a strong sculptural presence, this pitcher is an exquisite example of Danish design excellence and superlative craftsmanship.

992 pitcher, 1952

Henning Koppel (Denmark, 1918–1981)

www.georgjensen.com
Sterling silver
↕ 28.7 cm
Georg Jensen, Copenhagen, Denmark

During the 1920s, Kay Fisker sought to modernize Danish design through the creation of Art Deco silverware that prioritized strong geometric forms. In 1928, his work was awarded the Eckersberg Medal and, that same year, he designed this elegant pitcher, possessing an understated beauty bound to its functional purity. An exquisite Art Deco object, the *KF* presaged the more organic forms of the postwar era.

KF pitcher, 1928

Kay Fisker (Denmark, 1893–1965)

www.georgjensen.com
Sterling silver
↕ 25 cm
Georg Jensen, Copenhagen, Denmark

980A bowl, 1948

Henning Koppel (Denmark, 1918–1981)

www.georgjensen.com
Sterling silver
⌀ 39.5 cm
Georg Jensen, Copenhagen, Denmark

Henning Koppel started his career as a sculptor, notably
working with granite, but in 1945 he began creating jewellery for Georg Jensen in a far more malleable material:
silver. He subsequently designed home wares in silver for
the same company. Modelled into expressive and oozing
biomorphic forms – such as this exquisite solid silver bowl –
his designs fully exploited the plastic potential of this
beautiful and luminous metal.

1026 covered fish dish, 1954

Henning Koppel (Denmark, 1918–1981)

www.georgjensen.com
Sterling silver
↔ 68 cm
Georg Jensen, Copenhagen, Denmark

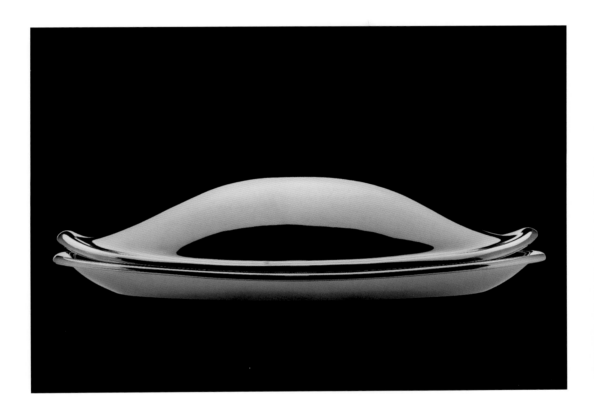

One of the most iconic designs produced by Georg Jensen, the *1026* covered fish dish is impressively large, being able to accommodate a sizeable salmon. It is also imposing as a sculptural object, with its gleaming surfaces emphasizing the flowing, gestural lines of its organic form. Like other designs by Henning Koppel, this design has an enduring appeal due to a sensual aesthetic that delights both hand and eye.

This decanter is an outstanding example not only of Danish glassmaking, but also of Henning Koppel's distinctively sculptural approach to design. Its sensuous and fluid form ensures that it pours beautifully, while its rounded curves also allow the wine to breathe properly, and so taste better – a perfect case of form enhancing function. The design can also be used as a water carafe, and even when not in use it is a truly beautiful object in its own right.

Henning Koppel decanter, 1970

Henning Koppel (Denmark, 1918–1981)

www.holmegaard.com
Glass
↕ 22 cm
Holmegaard Glasværk, Holmegaard, Denmark

925s wine decanter, 2004

Ole Palsby (Denmark, 1935–)

www.georgjensen.com
Glass, sterling silver
0.75 l, 1 l
Georg Jensen, Copenhagen, Denmark

Using a logical, hands-on approach to the design process, Ole Palsby hones his designs for housewares to such a level of perfection that they frequently meet his ultimate goal of looking, 'as natural as if the design had just occurred of its own accord'. For instance, his *925s* wine decanter for Georg Jensen, with its silver drip-catching lip, has an understated Scandinavian elegance that belies the extreme refinement of Palsby's evolutionary design methodology.

Riedel can trace its origins in northern Bohemian glass-making back to the 17th century. Indeed, eleven generations of the Riedel family have nurtured the company's development into the world's most renowned manufacturer of wine glasses. In recent years, the company has also developed several innovative decanters, including the lyre-shaped *Amadeo,* which is free-blown by master craftsmen using clear or black lead crystal.

Amadeo decanter, 2006

Stefan Umdash (Austria, 1963–)

www.riedel.com
Hand-blown lead crystal
↕ 35 cm 750 cl
Riedel Glas, Kufstein, Austria

Swan decanter, 2007

Georg Riedel (Austria, 1949–) & Maximilian Riedel (Austria, 1977–)

www.riedel.com
Hand-blown lead crystal
↕ 60 cm 1.5 l
Riedel Glas, Kufstein, Austria

With its elegantly slender and elongated neck, softly swelling body and upturned tail, the *Swan* decanter is not only a functional wine server but also a beautiful and sculptural object that would enhance any dining room sideboard. Like all decanters, the bird-inspired *Swan* exposes the wine, whether a fine vintage or a younger one, to more oxygen. This, in turn, allows it to reach its optimum, flavoursome potential.

LM-400 corkscrew, 2003

Screwpull Design Team

www.screwpull.com
Zamak (zinc-plated aluminium alloy)
Screwpull/Le Creuset, Fresnoy-le-Grand, France

Marketed by Screwpull as 'the best corkscrew in the world', the *LM-400* incorporates a patented rotational technology that allows bottles to be uncorked effortlessly just by raising and then lowering the design's handle-like lever. To remove the cork from the corkscrew is a similarly easy, two-stage 'up-down' action. Underwritten by a ten-year guarantee, this design also incorporates a non-stick coating on its screw section, and was specifically designed for removing synthetic corks.

LM-200 corkscrew, 1979

Screwpull Design Team

www.screwpull.com
Glass-reinforced polyamide
Screwpull/Le Creuset, Fresnoy-le-Grand, France

Invented in the late 1970s, the *LM-200* was the first lever-action corkscrew and, although its 'up-down' mechanism has often been copied, it has never been equalled in performance. In fact, the *LM-200* holds the Guinness world record for the greatest number of wine bottles opened in one minute: a total of eight. Its ergonomic design ensures a comfortable grip, while its incorporation of a non-stick coating guarantees that the screw glides through even the toughest cork.

Socrates corkscrew, 1998

Jasper Morrison (UK, 1959–)

www.alessi.com
Stainless steel
Alessi, Crusinallo, Italy

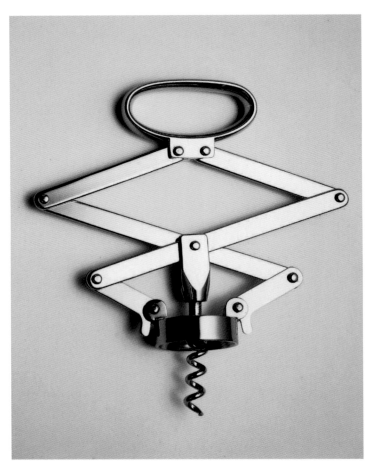

The *Socrates* corkscrew by Jasper Morrison might not be particularly ergonomic, but its fine engineering and thoughtful design certainly mean that it works well. Like other essentialist designs by Morrison, its functional purity and industrial aesthetic give it a distinctively masculine presence, and help to convey that this is no plaything but a tool that is resolutely fit for purpose.

Soft Machine corkscrew, 2006

L'Atelier du Vin Design Team

www.atelierduvin.com
Elastomer-coated ABS, metal
L'Atelier du Vin, Breteuil-sur-Noye, France

This patented design was created for the wine connoisseur who wants to open a vintage bottle without fear of damaging the cork. The *Soft Machine* has a unique gearing system that extracts the cork in one continuous movement: slicing through the foil with a cutting wheel positioned inside the lever arm, twisting the screw into the cork, and then releasing the cork with the handle's upward motion. Sommelierly simple.

Icebucket/Winecooler, 2005

Jakob Wagner (Denmark, 1963–)

www.menu.as
Stainless steel, plastic, glass
↕ 22.5 cm
Menu, Fredensborg, Denmark

Graceful yet practical, this design can either be used as a wine cooler or as a lidded ice bucket with matching ice-tongs. It efficiently keeps the cold in, while simultaneously collecting condensation. Like so many other Danish designs for the home, Jakob Wagner's Icebucket/Winecooler has a sophisticated elegance that derives from the country's longstanding tradition of design-engineering excellence.

5052 wine cooler, 1979

Ettore Sottsass (Italy, 1917–2007)

www.alessi.com
Polished stainless steel
↕ 23 cm
Alessi, Crusinallo, Italy

A contemporary interpretation of the traditional wine cooler, the *5052* by Ettore Sottsass has a gleaming, mirror-like outer surface of polished stainless steel, which subtly contrasts with its satin-finished interior. Large enough to accommodate two bottles of Sancerre, Chablis or champagne, this design is also deep enough for bottles to be cooled up to their necks. Moreover, its distinctive handles and rolled rim allow it to be carried easily with just one hand.

Sommeliers wine glasses, 1973

Claus Josef Riedel (Austria, 1925–2004)

www.riedel.com
Blow-moulded lead crystal
Riedel Glas, Kufstein, Austria

In 1973 the famous Austrian wine-glass-making company, Riedel launched its landmark *Sommeliers* range of ten wine glasses, which Claus Josef Riedel had designed with the assistance of the Associazione Italiana Sommerliers. For the first time, the design of each glass was based on the individual character of the wine it was meant to contain. Unlike traditional cut-crystal goblets, these unadorned long-stemmed glasses emphasized the qualities of their contents and in so doing helped to change the perception of wine, while also enhancing its taste.

L'Exploreur wine glass, 2000

L'Atelier du Vin Design Team

www.atelierduvin.com
Glass
L'Atelier du Vin, Breteuil-sur-Noye, France

This classic yet unique wine glass features an 'aroma line': a raised internal ridge that helps the wine to release its bouquet when swirled around in the glass for a couple of minutes. For restaurants, this means that their diners can enjoy a bottle of wine at its best, without the impracticalities of opening it an hour in advance to let it breathe. The same principle can, of course, be applied at home.

TAC 02 glassware, 2002

Rosenthal Creative Center (Germany, est. 1961)

www.rosenthal.de
Glass
Various sizes
Rosenthal, Selb, Germany

The inspiration for this graceful glassware comes from
Walter Gropius' earlier *TAC I* tea service, which epitomises the functional and aesthetic refinement of German
Modernism. The Rosenthal Creative Center – formerly
known as the Design Studio – was established in 1961 and
not only works with outside artists and designers, but
also creates designs of its own. Rosenthal's hallmark is to
combine contemporary form with timeless elegance, as
displayed in the *TAC 02* stemware range.

Illusion glassware, 1950s

Nils Landberg (Sweden, 1907–1991)

www.orrefors.com
Glass
Various sizes
Orrefors Kosta Boda, Orrefors, Sweden

Nils Landberg originally designed
this classic glassware range in the
1950s, and since then the collection has been expanded in order
to meet the demand for new types
of drinking glasses. In the 1980s
Olle Alberius added new glasses
for Burgundy and water, and more
recently Malin Lindahl has created
two extra-large glasses with
generous bowls that enhance the
bouquet and flavour of the wine
being served.

870 cocktail shaker, 1957

Luigi Massoni (Italy, 1930–) & Carlo Mazzeri (Italy, 1927–)

www.alessi.com
Polished stainless steel
0.25 l, 0.5 l
Alessi, Crusinallo, Italy

One of the first objects created for Alessi by outside designers, the *870* cocktail shaker is a classic Mid-Century design. It was Mazzeri and Massoni's first project for the company, and subsequently became one of its all-time bestsellers, with over 1.5 million units sold to date. Now found in countless bars across the world, this mirror-surfaced design is not only highly practical but also epitomizes the casual elegance of Italian design.

Cheese Dome, 2005

Helene Tiedemann (Sweden, 1960–)

www.sagaform.com
Hand-blown glass, oak
⌀ 18 cm
Sagaform, Borås, Sweden

Helene Tiedemann studied industrial design in London
before training as an architect in Stockholm. Today, she
runs her own Stockholm-based office specializing in interior,
retail and product design. Her sensual yet functional design
language gives her products, such as the *Cheese Dome* for
Sagaform, an engagingly soft-edged, human-centric quality.

Concept cheese dome, 2007

Jenaer Glas Design Team

www.jenaer-glas.com
Glass, stainless steel
↕ 12.9 cm
Jenaer Glas/Zwiesel Kristallglas, Zwiesel, Germany

The idea behind the *Concept* range produced by Jenaer Glas
was to create a number of essential 'basics' for everyday
use. The *Concept* cheese dome, for instance, was intended
to look good on a kitchen countertop, while simultaneously
harmonising with any tableware service so that it could also
be used when dining. In the tradition of Wilhelm Wagenfeld,
who designed for the company during the 1930s, this design
exhibits a timeless functional simplicity.

Duo de Coutellerie cheese knives, c. 2005

L'Atelier du Vin Design Team

www.atelierduvin.com
Stainless steel, wood
L'Atelier du Vin, Breteuil-sur-Noye, France

These two wooden-handled knives were designed to cut all types of cheese – the long and strong 'fine cutter' is perfect for slicing and stabbing soft or pressed cheeses, while the hatchet-like 'extra-strong cutter' copes easily with firm, hard or semi-soft cheeses. Their solid wood handles also have an excellent and reassuring grip. It is not surprising that a country that so reveres the art of cheese making, should have devised such excellent tools for eating it.

Lou Buré butter knife, 2008

Stéphane Rambaud (France, 1968–)

www.laguiole.com
Stainless steel, horn
Forge de Laguiole, Laguiole, France

Famous around the world for its distinctive folding knives
and cutlery, the Forge de Laguiole can trace its history back
to 1829. In that year, it produced its first knife, inspired by
a local fixed-blade design, as well as a traditional, folding
utility knife from Spain, known as a *Navaja*. Since then,
Laguiole has diversified its product line to include various
types of knives and household implements, including this
stylishly simple butter knife.

Cheese knife & cheese plane, 2007

Forge de Laguiole Design Team & Roland Barthélemy (France, 1949–)

www.laguiole.com
Stainless steel, juniper
Forge de Laguiole, Laguiole, France

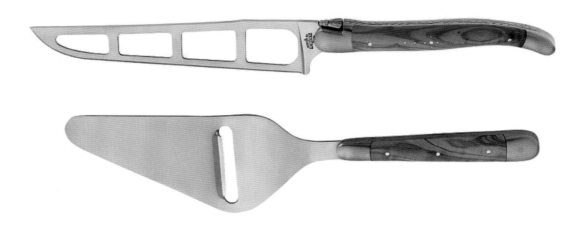

The French love of cheese is legendary, and so it is perhaps predictable that some of the best 'cheese tools' are manufactured in France. This cheese knife and plane were created in conjunction with Roland Barthélemy, the renowned master cheese maker and president of the Guilde des Fromagers (the guild of French cheese makers). The resulting implements are not only beautifully crafted but are also superior to use.

Collective Tools cheese knife & cheese slicer, 2000

Antonio Citterio (Italy, 1950–)
& Glen Oliver Löw (Germany, 1959–)

www.iittala.com
Stainless steel
Iittala, Iittala, Finland

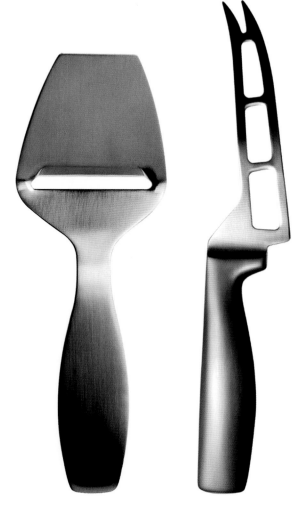

Made of satin-finish, high-grade stainless steel, Antonio Citterio and Glen Oliver Löw's cheese knife and cheese slicer belong to their *Collective Tools* range for Iittala – renowned for its distinctive styling and superb ergonomic handling. The handles of these useful 'tools for living' fit comfortably in the hand, and have a deeply satisfying sense of weighty balance.

Mingle three-piece cheese set, 2005

Peter Moritz (Sweden, 1964–) & Eva Moritz (Sweden, 1966–)

www.sagaform.com
Stainless steel
Sagaform, Borås, Sweden

Designed to compliment perfectly the *Mingle Lazy Susan* cheese-board, this three-piece set incorporates a slicer for hard cheeses, a sharp knife for semi-soft cheeses (such as Brie or Camembert) and a trowel-like implement for cream cheeses. Like most Scandinavian-designed objects for the home, these simple tools have an aesthetic and functional beauty derived from their respectful attentiveness to the requirements of everyday life.

One day, the Norwegian furniture maker Thor Bjørklund wanted to slice some cheese for a sandwich while in his carpentry shop. He decided to use his carpenter's plane, and was so impressed with the resulting even slivers of cheese that, in 1925, he designed a smaller, kitchen-sized version, thereby creating the world's first hand-held cheese slicer. When they saw how well it worked, his friends and relatives all wanted one too, which convinced Bjørklund that his idea was good enough to patent. The version shown here, based on Bjørklund's original design, is the best-selling model manufactured by the company he founded.

Allround-høvel cheese slicer, 1925

Thor Bjørklund (Norway, 1889–1975)

www.bjorklund-1925.no
Stainless steel, teak
Thor Bjørklund & Sønner, Lillehammer, Norway

Kartio tumblers, 1958

Kaj Franck (Finland, 1911–1989)

www.iittala.com
Pressed glass
Iittala, Iittala, Finland

Like his *Kilta* dinner service, Kaj Franck's *Kartio* glassware was intended for everyday use. Stackable and practical, this tumbler range and its matching pitcher were specifically designed to be mass-produced from clear pressed glass in a number of mix-and-match, earthy-toned colours. The range was christened *Kartio* in 1993, a Finnish word meaning 'cone' or 'taper' – highly appropriate considering its elemental, funnel-like form.

Classic tumblers, 1948

Freda Diamond (USA, 1905–1998)

www.libbey.com
Pressed glass
Libbey Glass, Toledo (OH), USA

In the early 1940s, and at the suggestion of Walter Dorwin Teague, Libbey glassworks hired a female design consultant, Freda Diamond. Two years later, Diamond commissioned a survey of consumer tastes, and used the resulting market research data to, as she put it, 'shape demand'. A strong advocate of 'good design', Diamond put theory into practice with her affordable, practical and stylish *Classic* tumblers, which are available in aqua, mocha, olive, smoked and clear glass.

Aalto glassware, 1932

Aino Aalto (Finland, 1894–1949)

www.iittala.com
Pressed glass
Iittala, Iittala, Finland

Aino Aalto, the wife and business partner of the famous
Finnish architect, Alvar Aalto was an accomplished designer
in her own right. This pressed glass set was initially
designed as a submission for a competition sponsored by
the Karhula-Iittala glassworks in 1932, where it won second
prize. Originally named *Bölgeblick*, which means 'wave view',
the chunkily ribbed *Aalto* range – comprising glasses, bowls,
plates and an elegant pitcher – revealed Aino's concern for
practicality and standardization in design.

Gibraltar tumblers, 1977

Libbey Glass New Products Development Group

www.libbey.com
Pressed glass
Libbey Glass, Toledo (OH), USA

Another seminal design manufactured by Libbey, the
Gibraltar pattern was inspired by a Baccarat tumbler that
Freda Diamond had seen on one of her many travels. This
range of large and robust utility glassware is a classic of
American design: a masculine, no-nonsense, durable and
chunky pattern for the everyman that eloquently reflects
the casual lifestyle and seemingly classless nature of
American society.

Aarne glassware, 1948

Göran Hongell (Finland, 1902–1973)

www.iittala.com
Mould-blown glass
Iittala, Iittala, Finland

One of the great pioneers of Finnish glass design, Göran Hongell was an artistic adviser to the Karhula glassworks during the 1930s. During the 1940s, he began to design glassware characterized by simplified forms and undecorated surfaces. His classic *Aarne* glassware has an innovative form that falls somewhere between a tumbler and a stemmed glass. While reassuringly chunky in the hand, it remains pleasing to the eye.

Tapio glassware, 1952

Tapio Wirkkala (Finland, 1915–1985)

www.iittala.com
Mould-blown glass
Iittala, Iittala, Finland

One of the most accomplished designers of all time, Tapio Wirkkala created sculpturally beautiful objects that possess breathtaking originality. The *Tapio* glassware range is a testament to his understanding of materials and natural forms, as well as to his mastery of glass-making techniques. It has an engaging, ice-like presence, and the air bubbles trapped inside the heavy stem of each glass are placed there through the skilful use of a wet stick.

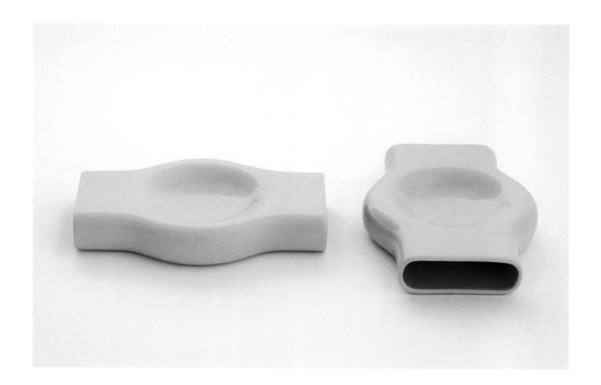

Smoky ashtray, 2007

Carlo Contin (Italy, 1967–)

www.sphaus.com
Glazed ceramic
SpHaus, Milan, Italy

This stylish ashtray works equally well as a change holder or key rest. Echoing the shapes found in Italian design during the 1960s, this is a Neo-Pop design that is just a really nice object to live with. Made from glazed ceramic, *Smoky* is available with a black or white exterior and interior options including red, fuchsia, yellow or orange. Highly sculptural, the design is also easy to pick up thanks to the handle-like projections set either side of its hollowed bowl.

Drinks coasters & stand, 1998

John Campbell (UK, 1943–)

www.jacampbell.co.uk
Sterling silver, maple wood
⌀ 9.5 cm
JA Campbell, Brentwood, UK

Over the decades, British design has often been characterised by a subtle refinement and understated elegance that is
exemplified in these beautifully simple yet highly functional
coasters. Made of sterling silver and maple, this exquisite
British-made set possesses an essentialist aesthetic that
gives it an enduring timeless quality.

486 napkin holder, 1997

Peter Holmblad (Denmark, 1934–)

www.stelton.com
Stainless steel
↔ 19 cm
Stelton, Copenhagen, Denmark

In Scandinavia there is a widespread belief that well-designed objects, especially those destined for the home, can enhance daily life. This would certainly explain the high-quality design engineering found in Peter Holmblad's remarkable products. His satin-polished stainless-steel *486* napkin holder, for example, is both rationally conceived and stylishly minimal. As such, it exemplifies the aesthetic purity and functional practicality of Danish design.

5071 Parmesan cheese cellar, 1978

Ettore Sottsass (Italy, 1917–2007)

www.alessi.com
Glass, polished stainless steel
↕ 10 cm ⌀ 11 cm
Alessi, Crusinallo, Italy

The quintessential Parmesan cheese holder, this design is ubiquitous in Italy – every *trattoria* on every corner seems to possess at least one. Conceived by Ettore Sottsass in the late 1970s, it was intended to compliment his classic *5070* condiment set, also produced Alessi. It has a capacity of twenty centilitres, which makes it easy to hold and ensures that just the right amount of grated Parmesan is stored at any one time.

5070 condiment set, 1978

Ettore Sottsass (Italy, 1917–2007)

www.alessi.com
Glass, polished stainless steel
↕ 17.5 cm ↔ 8 cm
Alessi, Crusinallo, Italy

The *5070* condiment set designed by Ettore Sottsass is a veritable Italian design icon and is used everywhere in Italy – in homes, cafés, bars and restaurants. Holding two large cruets for oil and vinegar, and two smaller shakers for salt and pepper, it is as practical as it is stylish. The silhouette of this engaging design almost conjures up a vision of a miniature cityscape, with its domed towers nestling in their handy holder.

SG64 Mami oil cruet, 2003

Stefano Giovannoni (Italy, 1954–)

www.alessi.com
Stainless steel, plastic
↕ 25 cm
Alessi, Crusinallo, Italy

Part of Stefano Giovannoni's extensive *Mami* cooking range for Alessi,
this oil cruet is a useful addition to
the kitchen as well as an attractive item in its own right. Its name,
which means 'mummy' in Italian,
reveals that the maternal female
body inspired its soft curvaceous
form. Able to contain up to sixty-
five centilitres of olive oil, this is a
really handy design to keep near
the hob or stovetop.

AC01 oil & vinegar set, 1984

Achille Castiglioni (Italy, 1918–2002)

www.alessi.com
Glass, polished stainless steel
↕ 16.5 cm
Alessi, Crusinallo, Italy

One of Achille Castiglioni's best-loved designs, the *AC01* oil and vinegar set reflects this design maestro's ability to create functionally resolved and visually engaging objects. The unusual angles of the dispensers create a sense of aesthetic tension, but also help them to pour easily and cleanly.

Mushroom salt & pepper mills, c.1963

William Bounds Design Team

www.wmboundsltd.com
Metal, acrylic
↕ 13.5 cm
William Bounds, Torrance (CA), USA

For the last forty years, William Bounds has, to the best of our knowledge, manufactured the finest salt and pepper mills in the world. Incorporating a patented three-step adjusting ring and milling mechanism, the mills crush rather than grind the salt and pepper into three different grades of coarseness. Additionally, because the system does not grind metal against metal, the mills last for decades. In fact, the company has never had to replace a single one – although it still offers a somewhat superfluous lifetime warranty.

Twin salt & pepper mill, 2007

Bodum Design Group

www.bodum.com
Acrylic, non-slip rubber
↕ 13 cm
Bodum, Triengen, Switzerland

This unusual combination grinder for salt and pepper won an iF product design award in 2007. The idea behind the design is, according to Bodum, to make 'your chef life easier. Its two-grinders-in-one approach lets you spice up your cooking with two easy twists'. If you turn the cap to the right you get pepper, and if you twist it to the left you get salt: a simply ingenious solution.

The Hungarian-born ceramicist Eva Zeisel emigrated to the United States in 1938, and has since become one of the country's most celebrated designers. Despite her advanced years, she continues to create timeless and sculptural designs for the home, such as these exquisite salt and pepper shakers for Nambé, which echo the form of her *Harmony* vase and look like two miniature bowling pins with their organic, hourglass form. As with other Nambé products, they are made from a highly polished metal alloy that accentuates their alluring contours.

Eva Zeisel salt & pepper shakers, 1999

Eva Zeisel (Hungary/USA, 1906–)

www.nambe.com
Nambé alloy
↕ 10.7 cm
Nambé, Santa Fe (NM), USA

Good Grips salt & pepper grinders, 2007–2008

Factors NY (USA, est. 1974)

www.oxo.com
Stainless steel, acrylic, plastic, ceramic
↕ 13.9 cm
OXO International, New York City (NY), USA

The *Good Grips* range includes numerous straightforward products that can be used by people from almost all age groups, and even by those suffering from conditions such as arthritis. These salt and pepper grinders, for instance, have soft, non-slip grips that are extremely comfortable to hold. Moreover, their ability to rest flat when inverted, and their easy-to-unscrew caps, mean that they are also much simpler to refill than conventional grinders. Their clear acrylic bodies also show at a glance how full they are.

Hobart nutcracker, 1964

Robert Welch (UK, 1930–2000)

www.welch.co.uk
Cast iron, stainless steel
↕ 15 cm
Robert Welch, Chipping Campden, UK

The highly effective, vice-like screw element of this robust yet stylish cast-iron nutcracker will defeat even the toughest nut. Impervious to the vagaries of time, this solid and weighty design is built to last. Its endearing, 'industrial craft' aesthetic is a characteristic shared by all of Robert Welch's numerous kitchenware designs.

Lokerovati platter, 1957

Kaj Franck (Finland, 1911–1989)

www.arabia.fi
Vitreous china
↔ 24 cm
Arabia, Iittala Group, Helsinki, Finland

Designed by Kaj Franck in the late 1950s, the *Lokerovati*
platter adorns many homes in Finland, where it is rightly
regarded as a design classic. Certainly it has a very Japanese aesthetic, with its origami-like form giving it a strong
graphic quality. Apart from its undeniable beauty, it is also
a very practical design that is perfect for the serving of
hors-d'œuvres.

Model No. 3180 & Model No. 3081 Babell stands, 1996

Hints-Wien (Austria, active 1990s)

www.koziol.de
Thermoplastic
↕ 35, 20.8 cm
Koziol, Erbach, Germany

An elegant modern reworking of a classic cake stand, the *Babell étagères* come in two sizes: the larger *Model No. 3180* is perfect for cookies, fruit or *canapés*; while the smaller *Model No. 3081* is ideal for chocolates, candies and *petit fours*. The three stacking parts can also be used separately, and come in five different colours – white, pink, green, black and red.

1002 oil table lamp, 1983

Erik Magnussen (Denmark, 1940–)

www.stelton.com
Stainless steel, glass
↕ 24 cm   ⌀ 13 cm
Stelton, Copenhagen, Denmark

A modern reworking of a traditional kerosene oil lamp, the
1002 table light provides a subtle
glow that promotes a warm and
relaxed mood – especially on a
dark winter's evening. Essentially
a two-part cylinder of satin-
polished stainless steel and milky
translucent glass, this modern-
yet-elegant design complements
other pieces in the Stelton range.
Burning the midnight oil can have a
practical purpose too; the lamp is
a useful standby in case of power
supply problems.

Em & Em candleholder, 2005

Bastiaan Arler (Netherlands, 1972–)

www.sphaus.com
Glazed ceramic
SpHaus, Milan, Italy

Among the thousands of tea-light holders available for purchase, Bastiaan Arler's *Em & Em* candleholder stands out. This is not only a result of the perfect undulating proportions that make it function so well as a centerpiece, but is also attributable to its two-way design that allows candles of two different diameters to be used depending on which way up you place it. The glazed ceramic *Em & Em* has a glossy surface and is available in black, white or red.

Kivi tea light holder, 1988

Heikki Orvola (Finland, 1943–)

www.iittala.com
Blow-moulded glass
Iittala, Iittala, Finland

Heikki Orvola's *Kivi* votive candleholder has remained popular for over twenty years, thanks to its pure and simple cylindrical form, and its rainbow choice of twenty-three colours. As its designer explains, 'When I got the commission, I knew what they [Iittala] wanted from me: a Scandinavian glass candleholder. I gave it some thought and then that "blunt piece of tubing" began to take shape in my mind…When I sketched the shape, I thought, that's it right there – the only right solution'.

Lotus tea light holder, 1993

Torben Jørgensen (Denmark, 1945–)

www.holmegaard.com
Glass
↕ 6.5, 7, 9 cm
Holmegaard Glasværk, Holmegaard, Denmark

One of the most popular designs produced by Holmegaard, the *Lotus* tea-light holder is created using a technique originally developed in the 1930s, in which molten glass is allowed to 'float' from the mould. Based on a classic flower shape, the resulting abstracted form has an engaging, ice-like quality. As Jørgensen notes: 'As an artist I get great satisfaction out of being able to create good everyday items that people can enjoy and with which they can give pleasure to others.'

Lantern candleholder, 1999

Harri Koskinen (Finland, 1970–)

www.iittala.com
Blow-moulded glass
↕ 19 cm
Iittala, Iittala, Finland

The highly respected Finnish designer, Harri Koskinen is blessed with an extraordinary ability to create essentialist products that have a quiet, restrained beauty. For example, his large *Lantern* candleholder is an accomplished modern reworking of a traditional storm lantern, stripped of all superfluous detailing to reveal a pure, function–driven form. Koskinen has also created a smaller tabletop version, shown here, which can be used with tea lights.

Hobart candlestick, 1962

Robert Welch (UK, 1930–2000)

www.welch.co.uk
Cast iron
Robert Welch, Chipping Campden, UK

This iconic 1960s candlestick design has recently been put back into small-scale production and is available in two sizes. It was Robert Welch's first cast iron design to incorporate what he described as 'curved flanged forms', which he later repeated in several of his other kitchenware designs. This weighty and robust design has a striking silhouette and helped to define the British 'Contemporary Look'.

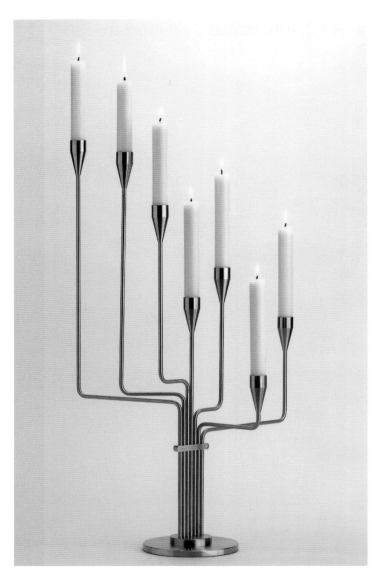

A rational idealist, an acclaimed mathematician and an award-winning designer, Piet Hein's proportionally harmonious products have a rare refinement born of true genius. During a trip to the Southern Hemisphere, Hein remarked how much he missed the Northern sky, and particularly the constellation known as The Great Bear. He was inspired to design this stunning candelabra, which has seven branches that can be adjusted into the position of the stars in 'Ursa Major' – or turn them in other directions to create a constellation of your own.

The Great Bear Candelabra, 1966

Piet Hein (Denmark, 1905–1996)

www.piethein.com
Stainless steel
↕ 63 cm
Piet Hein, Middelfart, Denmark

PO/9801A object-holder & PO/9801C candleholder, 1998

Tom Dixon (UK, 1959–)

www.cappellini.it
Silver-plated metal or polished copper
↕ 50 cm ↔ 50 cm ↗ 45 cm
Cappellini, Arosio, Italy

One of the most inventive and imaginative designers of his generation, Tom Dixon has always imbued his work with a visually distinctive craft sensibility. Dixon's sculptural *PO/9801A* and *PO/9801C* each have three bowl-like elements that can be used to store objects or hold candles respectively. Part of Cappellini's influential *Progetto Oggetto* collection, they also look wonderful if the tiered bowls are used to contain food, fruit or flowers.

Lucia candlestick, 1995

Thomas Sandell (Finland/Sweden, 1959–)

www.asplund.org
Polished aluminium
↕ 28 cm
Asplund, Stockholm, Sweden

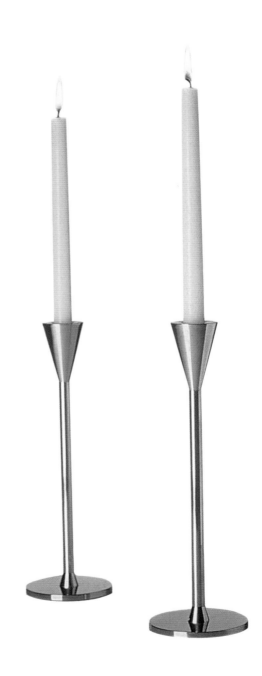

During the late 1980s and throughout the 1990s, there was a revival of design innovation in Scandinavia, with young designers exploring the impressive design legacy of their forefathers. They also created iconic designs of their own, often notable for their strong graphic quality. Thomas Sandell's *Lucia* candlesticks epitomize this phenomenon, and remain an elegant addition to any dining table or mantelpiece.

Crevasse vases, 2005

Zaha Hadid (Iraq/UK, 1950–)

www.alessi.com
Polished stainless steel
Alessi, Crusinallo, Italy

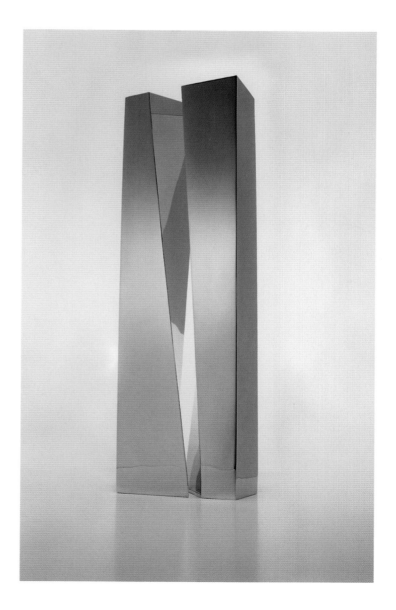

One of today's most visionary architects, Zaha Hadid has also recently turned her hand to the design of furniture, lighting and homewares. Her counterpoised *Crevasse* flower vases for Alessi are like two miniature skyscrapers, with their highly polished surfaces twisting upwards and reflecting each other. Like her buildings, these distinctive vases are formally progressive and have a strong sculptural presence.

Alvar Aalto Collection bowl, 1936

Alvar Aalto (Finland, 1898–1976)

www.iittala.com
Mould-blown glass
Iittala, Iittala, Finland

Alvar Aalto would never demonstrate how his glass objects should be used, desiring instead that people should decide for themselves. It is, perhaps, this freedom to interpret their function that has helped to keep the components of the *Aalto* collection so contemporary and fresh. The bowl that is shown here comes in various sizes and colours, and can also be used as a low vase. With its amorphous shape, this mould-blown bowl captures the abstract essence of nature, and recalls the ebbing of water along a shoreline.

Aalto vase, 1936

Alvar Aalto (Finland, 1898–1976)

www.iittala.com
Mould-blown glass
↕ 9.5, 12, 16 cm
Iittala, Iittala, Finland

Alvar Aalto created the *Aalto* vase in various shapes, sizes and colours for the World Fair in Paris in 1937 – including the *Savoy* version (shown below). Reputedly, the vase's form is based on sketches intriguingly titled, 'The Eskimo Woman's Leather Breeches'; but Aalto was also the son of a cartographer, so perhaps the shape could be derived from the Finnish landscape and lakes. One of the world's most famous and recognizable designs, the *Aalto* vase is a glorious example of Finnish art glass, and represents Alvar Aalto's influential and organic interpretation of Modernism.

Shape vase, 2005

Peter Svarrer (Denmark, 1957–)

www.holmegaard.com
Glass
↕ 17, 21 cm
Holmegaard Glasværk,
Holmegaard, Denmark

An accomplished glassware
designer, Peter Svarrer runs his
own glass studio in Vanløse,
Denmark. Since 1997, he has also
designed a large number of pieces
for Holmegaard, including his
exquisite, hand-blown *Shape* vase,
which is available in turquoise,
lime green, red, opal white, clear
and black. An archetypal design,
this vase provides the perfect,
eye-catching support for any floral
arrangement.

Harmony vase, 2001

Eva Zeisel (Hungary/USA, 1906–)

www.nambe.com
Nambé alloy
↕ 12.7 cm
Nambé, Santa Fe (NM), USA

This small vase, just five inches high, is perfect on a dining table because it requires so little space, while at the same time its powerful, sculptural presence still commands attention. With its curvaceous and organic form, *Harmony* suggests the abstracted shape of an unfurling bud about to blossom. The hand-polished metal alloy further accentuates the vase's harmonious proportions. This small and perfectly balanced design is testament to Eva Zeisel's esteemed position among the roster of design maestros.

Index

Picture credits

Aga, Telford: 138; Alessi, Crusinallo: 106, 113, 159, 182, 260, 263, 289, 290, 307; Alfi, Wertheim: 220, 221; All-Clad Metalcrafters, Canonsburg: 23, 32, 69, 79, 80, 81, 83, 96; Alpes-Inox, Bassano del Grappa: 149; Arabia/Iittala Group, Helsinki: 88, 296; Arzberg-Porzellan, Schirnding: 180, 195; Asplund, Stockholm: 306; Bambu, Mineola: 241; Bamix of Switzerland, Mettlen: 129; Bialetti Industrie, Coccaglio: 218; Blanco, Oberderdingen: 148; Bodum, Triengen: 14, 36, 38, 110, 204, 205, 292; Brabantia, Emmerlich: 112; Braun, Kronberg: 118, 119; Breville, Sydney: 127; Brita, Taunusstein: 115; Bulthaup, Bodenkirchen: 154, 155; C Hugo Pott/Seibel Designpartner, Mettmann: 170, 171; Cambro Manufacturing Company, Huntington Beach: 114; Cappellini, Arosio: 305; Chef's Choice/EdgeCraft, Avondale: 64; Covo, Formello: 210, 211, 234; Cuisipro, Markham: 10, 17, 20, 135; David Mellor, Sheffield: 176, 177, 178; Dualit, Crawley: 120; Eva Solo, Maaloev: 37; Famos-Westmark, Lennestadt: 28; © Fiell Image Archive: all images, photo: Paul Chave: 6, 15, 21, 25, 39, 46, 47, 62, 65, 70, 90, 91, 108, 109, 126, 133, 166, 207, 217, 219, 231, 269, 277, 278, 279, 281, 287, 288, 295; Figgjo, Figgjo: 194, 201, 216; Fiskars, Fiskars: 24; Forge de Laguiole, Laguiole: 103, 273, 274; Gateway Japan, Valby: 45, 71, 78, 156, 157, 192, 193; Gense, Eskilstuna: 1722, 173; Georg Jensen, Copenhagen: 158, 206, 225, 244, 250, 251, 252, 253, 255; Gustavsberg, Gustavsberg: 186; Hackman/Iittala Group, Iittala: 162; Hakusan Pottery Company, Nagasaki: 183; Holmegaard Glasværk, Holmegaard: 248, 249, 254, 301, 310; Iittala, Iittala: 86, 87, 89, 167, 179, 184, 185, 199, 246, 275, 280, 282, 283, 300, 302, 308, 309; Illy, Trieste: 124; JA Campbell, Brentwood: 285; Kenwood, Havant: 130; Kershaw Knives/Kai USA, Tualatin: 60; Kikkerland Design, New York: 33; KitchenAid, St Joseph: 131; Koziol, Erbach: 297; Kyocera, Kyoto: 8; L'Atelier du Vin, Breteuil-sur-Noye: 261, 265, 272; Le Creuset, Fresnoy-le-Grand: 84, 95; Legnoart, Omegna: 104, 105; Lifa Design, Holstebro: 152, 153; Magis, Motta di Livenza: 30, 136; Mauviel, Villedieu-les-Poêles: 4, 82, 92; Menu, Fredensborg: 262; Microplane International, Russellville: 16; Mono/Seibel Designpartner, Mettmann: 168, 169, 245; Nambé, Santa Fe: 230, 293, 311; Nestlé Nespresso, Paudex: 122, 123; Nikko/Idee, Tokyo: 213; Normann Copenhagen, Copenhagen: 31, 235; Norstaal, Bergen: 174, 175; Nouvel Studio, Naucalpan: 228; Orrefors Kosta Boda, Orrefors: 268; OXO International, New York: 40, 41, 53, 68, 97, 132, 134, 294; Piet Hein, Middelfart: 304; Pillivuyt, Mehun-sur-Yèvre: 93, 181; Riedel Glas, Kufstein: 256, 257, 264; Robert Welch, Chipping Campden: 303; Röstrand/Iittala Group, Höganäs: 188; Rosendahl, Hørsholm: 227; Rosenthal, Selb: 160, 161, 189, 190, 191, 214, 215, 229, 266, 267; Rösle, Marktoberdorf: 11, 18, 27, 42, 43 (both images); 48, 49, 72, 102, 107; Rowenta Werke, Offenbach am Main: 116, 117, 125; Royal Copenhagen, Copenhagen: 196, 197, 198, 200, 224; RSVP International, Seattle: 22, 29, 44, 111; Sagaform, Borås: 54, 55, 56, 57, 202, 236, 237, 242, 243, 270, 276; Sägi, Zurich: 58, 59; Samsung, Seoul: 146; Schott Jenaer Glas/Zwiesel Kristallgas, Zwiesel: 209, 232, 233, 271; Screwpull/Le Creuset, Fresnoy-le-Grand: 258, 259; Sfera, Kyoto: 208; Siemens, Munich: 121, 122; Simplehuman, Torrance: 137; SKK Küchen-und Gasgeräte, Viersen-Boisheim: 73, 74, 75; Smart Design, London: 12 (both images), 13 (both images), 50, 51, 52, 66, 67, 247; Smeg, Guastella: 142, 143; SpHaus, Milan: 284; Staub, Turckheim: 76, 77, 85, 94; Stelton, Copenhagen: 100, 100, 222, 223, 226, 286, 298; Sub-Zero Freezer Company, Madison: 147; Terraillon, Chatou Cedex: 34, 35; TG Green & Co, London: 187; Tonfisk Design, Turku: 212; Totally Bamboo, San Marcos: 238, 239, 240; Valcucine, Pordenone: 150, 151; Viking, Greenwood: 139, 140, 141, 144, 145; Vitra, Weil am Rhein: 203; Waring, Torrington: 128; WF Kaiser, Diez: 98; William Bounds, Torrance: 291; WMF Württembergische Metallwarenfabrik, Geislingen: 19, 163, 164, 165; Yoshida Metal Industry Company, Yoshida: 61; Zena, Affoltern: 9; Zeroll, Fort Pierce: 99; Zwilling JA Henckels, Solingen: 26, 63

Acknowledgements

This book has been a monumental undertaking and its realisation would not have been possible without the help and assistance of many people. Heartfelt thanks must firstly go to Jennifer Tilston for her excellent picture sourcing and good-natured perseverance. Special thanks must also go to Rob Payne and Mark Thomson for their first rate graphic design and tireless implementation, Paul Chave for his exquisite new photography, Quintin Colville for his superlative copy-editing and Rosanna Negrotti for her careful and precise proofreading. We would also like to give a very big thank you to the many designers and manufacturers who supplied images and information (you made this book happen!), including:

All-Clad – Chloe Faidy; Alessi – Pete Collard; Alias Design – Francesca Noseda; Arflex – Elisabette Bartesaghi; Artelano Paris – Raphäel Milan; Artemide – Dean Sahar; Artifort – Margiret van Sonsbeek; Arzberg – Ian Bailey; Asplund – Nina Brisius; Atelier du Vin – Simon Gilboy; Avarte – Noora Raitisto; B-Line – Fabio Bordin; B&B Italia – Laura Quickfall; Boffi – Ciara Philips; Cappellini/Poltrona Frau – Giuliana Reggio; Casala – Wilma Koning; Case Furniture – Duncan Bull; Cassina – Enrica Porro; Classicon – Alexandra Boeninger; Cuisipro – Elizabeth Burns; Danese – Laura Salviati; De La Espada – Phoebe Montoya; Dedon – Catherine Frinier; Driade – Francesco Farabola; Edra – Roberta Ugo; Emmemobili – Maurizio Rainoldi; Emu – Letizia Guardelli; Established & Sons – Juliet Scott; Erik Jorgensen – Charlotte Riis Røikjaer; Eva Solo – Majken Holmsteen; Flos – Clara Buoncristiani; Georg Jensen – Katrine Schrøder; Hans Grohe – Kayleigh; Herman Miller – Mike Stuk; Horm – Monica de Riz; Iittala – Sophie Linne; Isokon Plus – Cat; Jacob Jensen – Christopher Howie; Jasper Morrison – Laurence Maulderi; Kartell – Keren Avni; Knoll – Mabel Peralta; LaPalma – Maurizio Baiardo; Le Klint – Karin Frederiksen; Lifa Design – Merete Steenberg Thomsen; Louis Poulsen – Ida Praestgaard; Luxo – Romana Berzolla; Manufactum – Franziska Baumgaertner; Materia – Annica Gunnarsson; Matki – Helen Marsh; MDF Italia – Lucia Legè; Mobles 114 – Marta Termoleda; Modernica – Frank Novak; Moroso – Veronica Villa; Muji – James Lawless; Nendo – Akihiro Ito; OXO International – Charlotte Pinelli; Plank – Andreas Mangeng; Poliform – Sam Young; ProFeelDesign – Maarit Miettinen; Rosenthal – Silke Jahn; Royal Copenhagen – Karin Skipper-Ulstrup; RSVP – Cheryl Walczyk; Sagaform – Eva Fridén; Sanico – Estrella Sanz; SCP – Danka Nisevic; Serien – Helga Wiegel; Serralunga – Federica Moglia; Simplehuman – Rose Pater; Smart Design – Thomas Isaacson; SpHaus – Pamela Dell'Orto; Stelton – Nina Sylvest; String – Pär Josefsson; Stua – Jon Gasca; Swedese – Lina Fors; Theo Williams; Tobias Grau – Katherin Schmidtke; Vibia – James Mansfield; Vipp – Allan Sørensen; Vitra – Rahel Ueding; VitrA – Rebecca Wallace; Ycami – Silvia Marinoni & Nicoletta Galimberti; Zanotta – Daniela De Ponti; Zwilling – Brian Lane